Houghton
Mifflin
Harcourt

W9-COO-785

TEXAS
SCIENCE
fusion

fusion [FYOO • zhuhn] a combination of two
or more things that releases energy

This Write-In Student Edition belongs to

_____

Teacher/Room

_____

Consulting Authors

Michael A. DiSpezio
Global Educator
North Falmouth, Massachusetts

Marjorie Frank
*Science Writer and Content-Area Reading
    Specialist*
Brooklyn, New York

Michael Heithaus
*Executive Director, School of Environment, Arts, and
    Society*
*Associate Professor, Department of Biological
    Sciences*
Florida International University
North Miami, Florida

Donna Ogle
Professor of Reading and Language
National-Louis University
Chicago, Illinois

Front Cover: *lion* ©Cesar Lucas Abreu/Stone/Getty Images; *grass* ©Nicholas Eveleigh/Stockbyte/Getty Images; *tulips* ©John McAnulty/Corbis; *soccer* ©Jon Feingersh Photography Inc/Blend Images/Getty Images; *volcano* ©Westend 61 GmbH/Alamy; *microscope* ©Thom Lang/Corbis.

Back Cover: *guitar* ©Brand Z/Alamy; *giraffe* ©Nicholas Eveleigh/Stockbyte/Getty Images; *observatory* ©Robert Llewellyn/Workbook Stock/Getty Images; *wind turbine* ©Comstock/Getty Images.

Copyright © 2015 by Houghton Mifflin Harcourt Publishing Company

All rights reserved. No part of this work may be reproduced or transmitted in any form or by any means, electronic or mechanical, including photocopying or recording, or by any information storage and retrieval system, without the prior written permission of the copyright owner unless such copying is expressly permitted by federal copyright law. Requests for permission to make copies of any part of the work should be addressed to Houghton Mifflin Harcourt Publishing Company, Attn: Contracts, Copyrights, and Licensing, 9400 Southpark Center Loop, Orlando, Florida 32819-8647.

Printed in the U.S.A.

ISBN   978-0-544-02546-2

11   0928   20 19

4500742764   BCDEFG

If you have received these materials as examination copies free of charge, Houghton Mifflin Harcourt Publishing Company retains title to the materials and they may not be resold. Resale of examination copies is strictly prohibited.

Possession of this publication in print format does not entitle users to convert this publication, or any portion of it, into electronic format.

Program Advisors

Paul D. Asimow
Professor of Geology and Geochemistry
California Institute of Technology
Pasadena, California

Bobby Jeanpierre
Associate Professor of Science Education
University of Central Florida
Orlando, Florida

Gerald H. Krockover
Professor Emeritus of Earth, Atmospheric, and Planetary Science Education
Purdue University
West Lafayette, Indiana

Rose Pringle
Associate Professor School of Teaching and Learning
College of Education
University of Florida
Gainesville, Florida

Carolyn Staudt
Curriculum Designer for Technology
KidSolve, Inc.
The Concord Consortium
Concord, Massachusetts

Larry Stookey
Science Department
Antigo High School
Antigo, Wisconsin

Carol J. Valenta
Associate Director of the Museum and Senior Vice President
Saint Louis Science Center
St. Louis, Missouri

Barry A. Van Deman
President and CEO
Museum of Life and Science
Durham, North Carolina

Texas Reviewers

Max Ceballos
District Science Specialist
Edinburg, Texas

Tamara L. Cryar
Cook Elementary
Austin, Texas

Heather Domjan
University of Houston
Houston, Texas

Ashley D. Golden
Washington Elementary
Big Spring, Texas

Linda Churchwell Halliman
Cornelius Elementary School
Houston, Texas

Ellen Lyon
Hays Consolidated ISD
Kyle, Texas

Stephanie McNeil
Bastian Elementary
Houston, Texas

Sue Mendoza
District Science Coach
El Paso ISD
El Paso, Texas

Christine L. Morgan
Emerson Elementary
Midland, Texas

Genaro Ovalle III
Elementary Science Dean
Laredo ISD
Laredo, Texas

Hilda Quintanar
Science Coach
El Paso ISD
El Paso, Texas

Power up with Texas Science Fusion!

Grade 1

Your program fuses...

e-Learning & Virtual Labs

Labs & Explorations

Write-In Student Edition

... to generate new energy for today's science learner— **you.**

Write-In Student Edition

S.T.E.M.

Engineering and Technolog

STEM activities throughout the program!

Be an active reader and make this book your own!

Write your ideas, answer questions, make notes, and record activity results right on these pages.

Learn science concepts and skills by interacting with every page.

It's Your Mo...

Objects can move in many way... They can move in a straight line, ...back and forth, or round and rou...

...race the dashed lines below to ...ow the ways objects can move.

zigzag

e-Learning & Virtual Labs

Digital lessons and virtual labs provide e-learning options for every lesson of *Science Fusion*.

On your own or with a group, explore science concepts in a digital world.

Unit 2 **Technology All Around Us**

Lesson

How Do Engineers
Work?

Inquiry

How Can We
Solve a Problem?

Lesson

What Materials
Make Up Objects?

Inquiry

How
Materi
Sorte

Investigate every science
concept with multiple
virtual labs in every unit.

Continue your science explorations with these online tools:

- → ScienceSaurus
- → NSTA Scilinks
- → Video-based Projects

- → People in Science
- → Media Gallery
- → Vocabulary Cards

→ Science Readers for Texas with complete AUDIO!

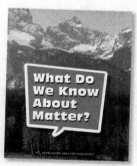

What Do We Know About Matter?

What Do We Know About Matter?

Making Crayons

Labs & Explorations

Science is all about doing.

Ask questions and test your ideas.

Draw conclusions and share what you learn.

How Are Plants of the Same Kind Different?

Observe plants to compare and contrast them. How are plants of the same kind different?

Materials
bunch of carrots

1 Observe the carrots to see how they are different. **Caution!** Do not eat the carrots.

2 Draw and write your observations.

3 Compare your drawings. How can carrots be different from one another?

Exciting investigations for every lesson.

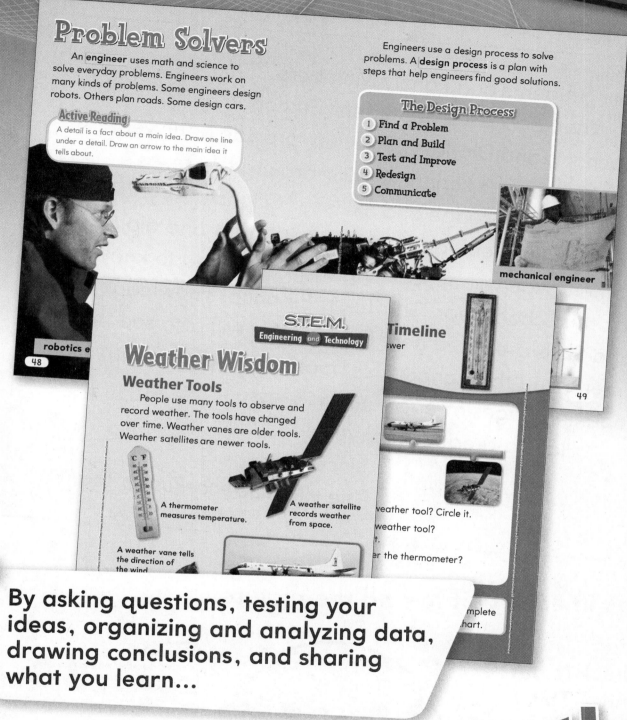

Problem Solvers

An **engineer** uses math and science to solve everyday problems. Engineers work on many kinds of problems. Some engineers design robots. Others plan roads. Some design cars.

Active Reading

A detail is a fact about a main idea. Draw one line under a detail. Draw an arrow to the main idea it tells about.

robotics e

48

Engineers use a design process to solve problems. A **design process** is a plan with steps that help engineers find good solutions.

The Design Process

1. Find a Problem
2. Plan and Build
3. Test and Improve
4. Redesign
5. Communicate

mechanical engineer

49

S.T.E.M.
Engineering and Technology

Weather Wisdom

Weather Tools

People use many tools to observe and record weather. The tools have changed over time. Weather vanes are older tools. Weather satellites are newer tools.

A thermometer measures temperature.

A weather satellite records weather from space.

A weather vane tells the direction of the wind.

Timeline

swer

weather tool? Circle it.

weather tool?

er the thermometer?

mplete
hart.

By asking questions, testing your ideas, organizing and analyzing data, drawing conclusions, and sharing what you learn...

You are the scientist!

Texas Essential Knowledge and Skills

Dear Students and Family Members,

The *ScienceFusion* Student Edition, Inquiry Flipchart, and Digital Curriculum provide a full year of interactive experiences built around the Texas Essential Knowledge and Skills for Science. As you read, experiment, and interact with print and digital content, you will be learning what you need to know for this school year. The Texas Essential Knowledge and Skills are listed here for you. You will also see them referenced throughout this book. Look for them on the opening pages of each unit and lesson.

Have a great school year!

Sincerely,
The HMH *ScienceFusion* Team

Look in each unit to find the picture.

Check it out:
Unit 5 This picture is found on page ____.

TEKS 1.1

Scientific investigation and reasoning. The student conducts classroom and outdoor investigations following home and school safety procedures and uses environmentally appropriate and responsible practices. The student is expected to:

A recognize and demonstrate safe practices as described in the Texas Safety Standards during classroom and outdoor investigations, including wearing safety goggles, washing hands, and using materials appropriately;

B recognize the importance of safe practices to keep self and others safe and healthy; and

C identify and learn how to use natural resources and materials, including conservation and reuse or recycling of paper, plastic, and metals.

Answer Key: page 182

© Houghton Mifflin Harcourt Publishing Company (bc) © Bets LaRue/Alamy

Check it out:
Unit 1 This picture is found on page ____.

Check it out:
Unit 2 This picture is found on page ____.

Check it out:
Unit 6 This picture is found on page ____.

TEKS 1.2

Scientific investigation and reasoning.
The student develops abilities to ask questions and seek answers in classroom and outdoor investigations. The student is expected to:

A ask questions about organisms, objects, and events observed in the natural world;

B plan and conduct simple descriptive investigations such as ways objects move;

C collect data and make observations using simple equipment such as hand lenses, primary balances, and non-standard measurement tools;

D record and organize data using pictures, numbers, and words; and

E communicate observations and provide reasons for explanations using student-generated data from simple descriptive investigations.

TEKS 1.3

Scientific investigation and reasoning.
The student knows that information and critical thinking are used in scientific problem solving. The student is expected to:

A identify and explain a problem such as finding a home for a classroom pet and propose a solution in his/her own words;

B make predictions based on observable patterns; and

C describe what scientists do.

TEKS 1.4

Scientific investigation and reasoning.
The student uses age-appropriate tools and models to investigate the natural world. The student is expected to:

A collect, record, and compare information using tools, including computers, hand lenses, primary balances, cups, bowls, magnets, collecting nets, notebooks, and safety goggles; timing devices, including clocks and timers; non-standard measuring items such as paper clips and clothespins; weather instruments such as classroom demonstration thermometers and wind socks; and materials to support observations of habitats of organisms such as aquariums and terrariums; and

B measure and compare organisms and objects using non-standard units.

© Houghton Mifflin Harcourt Publishing Company   (cr) Pierre BRYE/Alamy

Answer Key: page 26, page 59, page 240

**Check it out:
Unit 3** This picture is found on page ____.

**Check it out:
Unit 4** This picture is found on page ____.

**Check it out:
Unit 5** This picture is found on page ____.

TEKS 1.5

Matter and energy. The student knows that objects have properties and patterns. The student is expected to:

A classify objects by observable properties of the materials from which they are made such as larger and smaller, heavier and lighter, shape, color, and texture; and

B predict and identify changes in materials caused by heating and cooling such as ice melting, water freezing, and water evaporating.

TEKS 1.6

Force, motion, and energy. The student knows that force, motion, and energy are related and are a part of everyday life. The student is expected to:

A identify and discuss how different forms of energy such as light, heat, and sound are important to everyday life;

B predict and describe how a magnet can be used to push or pull an object;

C describe the change in the location of an object such as closer to, nearer to, and farther from; and

D demonstrate and record the ways that objects can move such as in a straight line, zig zag, up and down, back and forth, round and round, and fast and slow.

TEKS 1.7

Earth and space. The student knows that the natural world includes rocks, soil, and water that can be observed in cycles, patterns, and systems. The student is expected to:

A observe, compare, describe, and sort components of soil by size, texture, and color;

B identify and describe a variety of natural sources of water, including streams, lakes, and oceans; and

C gather evidence of how rocks, soil, and water help to make useful products.

© Houghton Mifflin Harcourt Publishing Company   (cl) ©Reed Kaestner/Corbis;   (cr) ©Frank Krahmer/Corbis

Answer Key: page 111, page 163, page 204

Check it out:
Unit 7 This picture is found on page ____.

Check it out:
Unit 8 This picture is found on page ____.

Check it out:
Unit 9 This picture is found on page ____.

TEKS 1.8

Earth and space. The student knows that the natural world includes the air around us and objects in the sky. The student is expected to:

A record weather information, including relative temperature, such as hot or cold, clear or cloudy, calm or windy, and rainy or icy;

B observe and record changes in the appearance of objects in the sky such as clouds, the Moon, and stars, including the Sun;

C identify characteristics of the seasons of the year and day and night; and

D demonstrate that air is all around us and observe that wind is moving air.

TEKS 1.9

Organisms and environments. The student knows that the living environment is composed of relationships between organisms and the life cycles that occur. The student is expected to:

A sort and classify living and nonliving things based upon whether or not they have basic needs and produce offspring;

B analyze and record examples of interdependence found in various situations such as terrariums and aquariums or pet and caregiver; and

C gather evidence of interdependence among living organisms such as energy transfer through food chains and animals using plants for shelter.

TEKS 1.10

Organisms and environments. The student knows that organisms resemble their parents and have structures and processes that help them survive within their environments. The student is expected to:

A investigate how the external characteristics of an animal are related to where it lives, how it moves, and what it eats;

B identify and compare the parts of plants;

C compare ways that young animals resemble their parents; and

D observe and record life cycles of animals such as a chicken, frog, or fish.

© Houghton Mifflin Harcourt Publishing Company; (c) Tanya Constantine/Getty Images; (cr) ©Steve Bloom Images/Alamy

Contents

Levels of Inquiry Key ■ DIRECTED ■ GUIDED ■ INDEPENDENT

Safety in Science xxiii
Inquiry Flipchart pp. 1–2—Safety in Science

THE NATURE OF SCIENCE AND S.T.E.M.

Unit 1—How Scientists Work. 1

Lesson 1 What Are Senses?. 3
Inquiry Flipchart p. 3—Shoebox Senses/All Around Me

Inquiry Lesson 2 How Can We Use Our Senses? 11
Inquiry Flipchart p. 4—How Can We Use Our Senses?

Lesson 3 What Are Inquiry Skills?. 13
Inquiry Flipchart p. 5—Measure Up/Animal Models

Inquiry Lesson 4 How Do We Use Inquiry Skills?. 23
Inquiry Flipchart p. 6—How Do We Use Inquiry Skills?

Lesson 5 What Are Science Tools?. 25
Inquiry Flipchart p. 7—It's Time to Measure/Balancing Act
Inquiry Flipchart pp. 8–9—Science Tools Activities

Lesson 6 How Do Scientists Work?. .35
Inquiry Flipchart p. 10—Holding Water/My Fingerprints

People in Science: Mary Anderson 45

Unit 1 Review 47

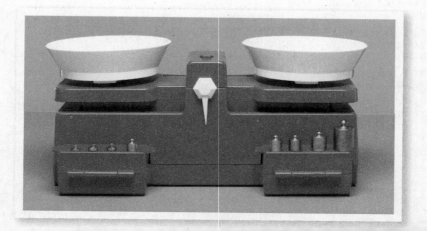

© Houghton Mifflin Harcourt Publishing Company

Unit 2—Technology All Around Us 51

Lesson 1 How Do Engineers Work? 53
Inquiry Flipchart p. 11—Don't Crack Up!/Make It Fly!

Inquiry Lesson 2 How Can We Solve a Problem? 65
Inquiry Flipchart p. 12—How Can We Solve a Problem?

Lesson 3 What Materials Make Up Objects? 67
Inquiry Flipchart p. 13—Build It!/Materials Mission

Inquiry Lesson 4 How Can Materials Be Sorted? 79
Inquiry Flipchart p. 14—How Can Materials Be Sorted?

People in Science: Dr. Eugene Tsui 81

Unit 2 Review 83

© Houghton Mifflin Harcourt Publishing Company · (t) ©Image Source/Getty Images

PHYSICAL SCIENCE
Unit 3—Matter 87

Lesson 1 What Can We Observe About Objects? 89
Inquiry Flipchart p. 15—Sort It Out!/What's the Weight?

Careers in Science: Polymer Scientist 101

Inquiry Lesson 2 How Can We Measure Temperature? 103
Inquiry Flipchart p. 16—How Can We Measure Temperature?

Lesson 3 How Does Heating and Cooling Change Matter? 105
Inquiry Flipchart p. 17—Water to Gas/Water Changes

S.T.E.M. Engineering and Technology: Kitchen Technology 115
Inquiry Flipchart p. 18—Think About Process: Write a Recipe

Unit 3 Review 117

© Houghton Mifflin Harcourt Publishing Company   (b) ©R. Morley/PhotoLink/Photodisc/Getty Images

Unit 4—Forces and Energy 121

Lesson 1 How Do We Use Energy? 123
Inquiry Flipchart p. 19—Making Toast/My Energy Survey

Lesson 2 How Do Magnets Move Objects? 135
Inquiry Flipchart p. 20—Push and Pull/Which Magnet Will Win?

Lesson 3 How Do Objects Move? 145
Inquiry Flipchart p. 21—Marble Race/Testing Toys

People in Science: Isaac Newton 153

Inquiry Lesson 4 How Can We Move a Ball? 155
Inquiry Flipchart p. 22—How Can We Move a Ball?

Lesson 5 How Can We Change the Way Objects Move? 157
Inquiry Flipchart p. 23—Changing Motion/Changing Location

S.T.E.M. Engineering and Technology: Fly to the Sky 169
Inquiry Flipchart p. 24—Build It: Paper Airplanes

Unit 4 Review 171

©Houghton Mifflin Harcourt Publishing Company (b) ©Martin Holtkamp/Getty Images

EARTH SCIENCE

Unit 5—Earth's Resources 175

Lesson 1 What Can We Find on Earth? 177
`Inquiry Flipchart` p. 25—Just Add Water/Resources All Around

People in Science: Dr. George Washington Carver 187

Lesson 2 What Is Soil? 189
`Inquiry Flipchart` p. 26—Cleaning Crew/How Much Water?

Inquiry Lesson 3 What Do We Find in Soil? 199
`Inquiry Flipchart` p. 27—What Do We Find in Soil?

Inquiry Lesson 4 How Do Soils Differ? 201
`Inquiry Flipchart` p. 28—How Do Soils Differ?

Lesson 5 Where Can We Find Water? 203
`Inquiry Flipchart` p. 29—Pass the Salt?/Water Watch

S.T.E.M. Engineering and Technology: Technology and the Environment 215
`Inquiry Flipchart` p. 30—Design It: Water Filter

Lesson 6 How Can We Save Resources? 217
`Inquiry Flipchart` p. 31—Trash on the Grass/Ready, Set, Recycle!

Unit 5 Review 229

© Houghton Mifflin Harcourt Publishing Company   (b) ©Frans Lanting/Corbis

Unit 6—Weather and Seasons 233

Lesson 1 What Is Weather? 235
Inquiry Flipchart p. 32—Hot or Cold?/Windsock Workshop

Inquiry Lesson 2 What Can We Observe About Weather? 247
Inquiry Flipchart p. 33—What Can We Observe About Weather?

People in Science: June Bacon-Bercey 251

Lesson 3 What Are Seasons? 253
Inquiry Flipchart p. 34—Keeping Warm/Turn Over a New Leaf

S.T.E.M. Engineering and Technology: Weather Wisdom 265
Inquiry Flipchart p. 35—Build It: Rain Gauge

Unit 6 Review 267

© Houghton Mifflin Harcourt Publishing Company   (b) ©Dennis MacDonald/Alamy Images

Unit 7—Objects in the Sky 271

Lesson 1 What Can We See in the Sky? 273
Inquiry Flipchart p. 36—High in the Sky/Star Fun

People in Science: Galileo Galilei 283

Lesson 2 How Does the Sky Seem to Change? 285
Inquiry Flipchart p. 37—Cloud Time/Moon and Stars Calendar

Inquiry Lesson 3 How Does the Sun Seem to Move? 295
Inquiry Flipchart p. 38—How Does the Sun Seem to Move?

S.T.E.M. Engineering and Technology: See the Light 297
Inquiry Flipchart p. 39—Design It: Lights for a Park

Unit 7 Review 299

LIFE SCIENCE
Unit 8—Living Things and Their Environments 303

Lesson 1 What Are Living and Nonliving Things? 305
Inquiry Flipchart p. 40—It's Alive!/Neighborhood Search

Lesson 2 Where Do Plants and Animals Live? 315
Inquiry Flipchart p. 41—Build an Aquarium/Working Together

Careers in Science: Forest Ranger 329

Inquiry Lesson 3 What Is a Terrarium? 331
Inquiry Flipchart p. 42—What Is a Terrarium?

S.T.E.M. Engineering and Technology: A Place for Animals 333
Inquiry Flipchart p. 43—Design It: Butterfly Garden

Unit 8 Review 335

© Houghton Mifflin Harcourt Publishing Company

Unit 9—Animals 339

Lesson 1 How Do Animals Differ? 341
Inquiry Flipchart p. 44—Animals Adapt/Picture Walk Safari

Inquiry Lesson 2 How Can We Group Animals? 353
Inquiry Flipchart p. 45—How Can We Group Animals?

S.T.E.M. Engineering and Technology: On the Farm 357
Inquiry Flipchart p. 46—Design It: Guard the Lettuce!

Lesson 3 What Are Some Animal Life Cycles? 359
Inquiry Flipchart p. 47—Where's the Caterpillar?/What's My Life Cycle?

Careers in Science: Zoo Keeper 371

Unit 9 Review 373

© Houghton Mifflin Harcourt Publishing Company (t) © Carsten Kooyman/Corbis

Unit 10—Plants 377

Lesson 1 What Are Some Parts of Plants? 379
Inquiry Flipchart p. 48—Are All Seeds Alike?/What Parts Do You See?

(i) **People in Science:** Dr Norma Alcantar 389

Lesson 2 How Are Plants Different? 391
Inquiry Flipchart p. 49—Rubbed Leaf Collection/Fantastic Flowers

Inquiry Lesson 3 How Can We Compare Leaves? 401
Inquiry Flipchart p. 50—How Can We Compare Leaves?

S.T.E.M. **Engineering and Technology:** Warm It Up 403
Inquiry Flipchart p. 51—Design It: Greenhouse

Unit 10 Review 405

Interactive Glossary R1

Index R21

© Houghton Mifflin Harcourt Publishing Company (b) ©Image Source/Corbis

Safety in Science

© Houghton Mifflin Harcourt Publishing Company ©PhotoObjects.net/Jupiterimages/Getty Images; (t) ©Chris Ryan/OJO Images/Getty Images

Indoors Doing science is fun. But a science lab can be dangerous. Know the safety rules and listen to your teacher.

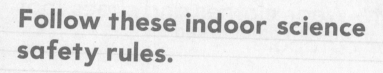

Follow these indoor science safety rules.

1. **Think ahead.** Study the steps. Follow them.

2. **Be neat.** Wipe up spills right away. Keep hair and clothing out of the way.

3. **Oops!** Tell your teacher if you spill or break something or if you get hurt.

4. **Watch your eyes.** Wear safety goggles when the teacher tells you.

5. **Ouch!** Do not touch sharp things.

6. **Yuck!** Do not eat or drink things.

7. **Don't get shocked.** Do not touch electric outlets.

8. **Keep it clean.** Clean up afterward. Wash your hands.

Outdoors Lots of science happens outdoors. Exploring the wilderness or your backyard is fun! But you need to be careful.

Follow these outdoor science safety rules.

1. **Think ahead.** Study the steps. Follow them.

2. **Dress right.** Wear clothes and shoes that are right for outdoors.

3. **Cover up.** Follow sun safety rules.

4. **Oops!** Tell your teacher if you break something or get hurt.

5. **Watch your eyes.** Tell your teacher right away if anything gets in your eyes. Wear goggles when your teacher tells you.

6. **Yuck!** Never taste anything outdoors.

7. **Stay together.** Stay on marked trails.

8. **Do not act wild.** No horseplay or pranks.

9. **Always walk.** No running!

10. **Clean up the area.** Throw away litter as your teacher tells you.

11. **Clean up.** Wash your hands with soap and water when you are done.

© Houghton Mifflin Harcourt Publishing Company ©PhotoObjects.net/Jupiterimages/Getty Images; (t) ©Monty Rakusen/Cultura Creative/Alamy Images

How Scientists Work

© Houghton Mifflin Harcourt Publishing Company ©Craig van der Lende/Photographer's Choice/Getty Images; ©E. Bhujim, MD/Photo Researchers/Getty Images

Big Idea

Scientists use inquiry skills and tools to help them find out information.

TEKS 1.2A, 1.2B, 1.2C, 1.2D, 1.2E, 1.3C, 1.4A, 1.4B

aquariums in Texas

I Wonder Why

Scientists study ocean animals. Why?
Turn the page to find out.

Here's Why Scientists study ocean animals and other animals to learn about how they live.

In this unit, you will explore this Big Idea, the Essential Questions, and the Investigations on the Inquiry Flipchart.

Levels of Inquiry Key ■ DIRECTED ■ GUIDED ■ INDEPENDENT

Track Your Progress

Big Idea Scientists use inquiry skills and tools to help them find out information.

Essential Questions

Lesson 1 What Are Senses? 3
Inquiry Flipchart p. 3—Shoebox Senses/All Around Me

Inquiry Lesson 2 How Can We Use Our Senses? 11
Inquiry Flipchart p. 4—How Can We Use Our Senses?

Lesson 3 What Are Inquiry Skills? 13
Inquiry Flipchart p. 5—Measure Up/Animal Models

Inquiry Lesson 4 How Do We Use Inquiry Skills? 23
Inquiry Flipchart p. 6—How Do We Use Inquiry Skills?

Lesson 5 What Are Science Tools? 25
Inquiry Flipchart p. 7—It's Time to Measure/Balancing Act
pp. 8–9—Science Tools Activities

Lesson 6 How Do Scientists Work? 35
Inquiry Flipchart p. 10—Holding Water/My Fingerprints

People in Science: Mary Anderson 45

Unit 1 Review 47

Now I Get the Big Idea!

Science Notebook

Before you begin each lesson, be sure to write your thoughts about the Essential Question.

© Houghton Mifflin Harcourt Publishing Company ©Craig van der Lende/Photographer's Choice/Getty Images ©G. Dimijian, MD/Photo Researchers/Getty Images

Essential Question

What Are Senses?

Engage Your Brain!

Find the answer to the question in the lesson.

Which sense is this child trying <u>not</u> to use?

the sense of

_____

Active Reading

Lesson Vocabulary
1. Preview the lesson.
2. Write the vocabulary term here.

_____

© Houghton Mifflin Harcourt Publishing Company

Your Senses

How do you learn about things? You use your five senses. Your **senses** are the way you learn about the world. The senses are sight, hearing, smell, taste, and touch. You use different body parts for different senses.

Active Reading

The main idea is the most important idea about something. Draw two lines under the main idea.

You hear with your ears.

© Houghton Mifflin Harcourt Publishing Company

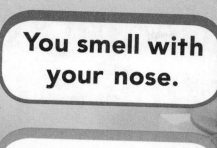

You smell with your nose.

You taste with your mouth.

You touch with your hands and skin.

You see with your eyes.

▶ Read the captions. Circle the name of the body parts you use for each sense.

© Houghton Mifflin Harcourt Publishing Company

Learning with Your Senses

How can your senses help you learn?
Look at the pictures. What would your
senses tell you about each thing?

Touching
You touch to learn about
texture—how things feel.

Hearing
You listen to learn
how things sound.

▶ Read the captions.
Underline how you learn
how things feel.

© Houghton Mifflin Harcourt Publishing Company

Seeing

You use sight to observe color, shape, and size.

Smelling

You use smell to learn how things smell.

Tasting

You taste to learn if foods are sweet, sour, or salty.

▶ Read the captions. You use sight to observe three things. Circle the words.

© Houghton Mifflin Harcourt Publishing Company

Sum It Up!

1 Choose It!

Circle the words that name parts of the body. Underline the words that name senses.

nose	touch	smell
taste	eyes	mouth

2 Match It!

Look at each thing. Which sense helps you learn about it? Draw lines to match them.

You touch to feel how furry something is.

You see to read.

You smell food baking.

© Houghton Mifflin Harcourt Publishing Company

Name _____

Word Play

You use different body parts for different senses. Label each body part with its sense.

| hearing | sight | smell | taste | touch |

© Houghton Mifflin Harcourt Publishing Company

Apply Concepts

Draw a line to the word that describes each sense.

hearing	hard
touching	loud
seeing	red
smelling	salty
tasting	fresh

Take It Home!

Family Members: Ask your child to tell how we use senses to learn about the world. Play a game to name the senses you use in different situations.

© Houghton Mifflin Harcourt Publishing Company

TEKS **1.2A** ask questions about organisms, objects, and events observed the natural world **1.2B** plan and condu simple descriptive investigations such as ways objects move **1.2D** record and organize data using pictures, numbers, a words

Name _____

Essential Question

How Can We Use Our Senses?

Set a Purpose

Tell what you want to find out.

_____

Think About the Procedure

❶ What will you observe?

_____

_____

❷ How will you find out the sound of breaking celery?

_____

© Houghton Mifflin Harcourt Publishing Company

Record Your Data

n this chart, write to record what you observe.

Sense	Observation
Sight	
Touch	
Smell	
Hear	
Taste	

Draw Conclusions

What did you find out about celery? How do you know?

_____

_____

Ask More Questions

What other questions could you ask about celery and your senses?

_____

_____

© Houghton Mifflin Harcourt Publishing Company

TEKS **1.2D** record and organize data using pictures, numbers, and words **1.2E** communicate observations and provide reasons for explanations using student-generated data from simple descriptive investigations

Essential Question

What Are Inquiry Skills?

Engage Your Brain!

Find the answer to the question in the lesson.

What can you infer this boy is doing?

The boy is

_____ .

Active Reading

Lesson Vocabulary

1 Preview the lesson.

2 Write the vocabulary term here.

_____

© Houghton Mifflin Harcourt Publishing Company ©Michael DeYoung/Corbis

Skills to Help You Learn

Observe and Compare

How can you be like a scientist? You can use inquiry skills. **Inquiry skills** help you find out information. They help you learn about your world.

Active Reading

You can compare things. You find ways they are alike. A child on this page is comparing two things. Draw a triangle around the two things.

Falling Leaves Forest

observe

compare

© Houghton Mifflin Harcourt Publishing Company

Predict and Measure

I predict that it is going to rain today.

measure

predict

Rocky Cliff

▶ Read the labels. Circle the inquiry skill that helps you find the size of an object.

© Houghton Mifflin Harcourt Publishing Company

Classify and Communicate

classify

Bird Paradise

▶ Complete the graph. Record how many brown birds there are.

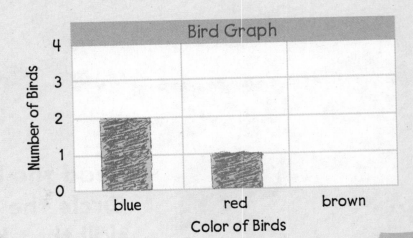

communicate

© Houghton Mifflin Harcourt Publishing Company

Hypothesize and Plan an Investigation

A big log rolls farther than a small log because it is heavier.

I will roll both logs down the hill to test the hypothesis.

hypothesize

plan an investigation

Rolling Logs Hill

▶ Look at the picture. Which child made a hypothesis? Draw a line under the hypothesis.

© Houghton Mifflin Harcourt Publishing Company

Infer and Draw Conclusions

I think the
light container
is empty.

Picnic
Palace

infer

Empty containers
are lighter than
full containers.

draw conclusions

▶ Read the captions.
Underline the
conclusion the
child drew.

18

© Houghton Mifflin Harcourt Publishing Company

Make a Model and Sequence

Butterfly Garden

▶ Look at the picture. Things may happen in order.
Write 1 beside what happens first.
Write 2 beside what happens second.
Write 3 beside what happens third.
Write 4 beside what happens last.

make a model

sequence _____

© Houghton Mifflin Harcourt Publishing Company

Sum It Up!

① Circle It!

You want to learn about something. Circle what you do to find out.

predict

classify

plan an investigation

② Choose It!

What inquiry skill does this show?

communicate

make a model

sequence

③ Draw It!

Observe an object. Draw it. Tell about it.

This is a _____. It is _____.

© Houghton Mifflin Harcourt Publishing Company

Name _____

Word Play

Circle the letters to spell the words.
Then complete the sentence.

compare	classify	infer	measure
observe	predict	sequence	

```
s    s  e  q  u  e  n  c  e  a
v    c  l  a  s  s  i  f  y
u    l  r  i  n  f  e  r  t
r    m  e  a  s  u  r  e  p
o    b  s  e  r  v  e  g  e
e    w  p  r  e  d  i  c  t
c    o  m  p  a  r  e  t  z
```

All the words in the puzzle
are _____ .

© Houghton Mifflin Harcourt Publishing Company

Apply Concepts

Circle the word that matches the meaning.

①	tell what you learn	communicate	observe
②	sort things into groups	sequence	classify
③	tell how things are alike and different	make a model	compare
④	put things in order	sequence	hypothesize
⑤	find out how much or how long	measure	infer
⑥	use your senses	make a model	observe
⑦	make a good guess about what will happen	predict	sequence
⑧	decide what steps to follow	draw conclusions	plan an investigation

Take It Home!

Family Members: Discuss with your child how inquiry skills are used around the home. For example, you measure when you cook and classify when you sort laundry.

© Houghton Mifflin Harcourt Publishing Company

Inquiry Flipchart p. 6

TEKS **1.2A** ask questions about organisms, objects, and events observed the natural world **1.2B** plan and conduct simple descriptive investigations such as ways objects move **1.2D** record and organize data using pictures, numbers, an words

Name _____

Essential Question

How Do We Use Inquiry Skills?

Set a Purpose

Tell what you want to find out.

_____

_____

_____

Think About the Procedure

1 What fair test did you plan? Write your plan here.

_____

_____

2 What science tools will you use for your test?

_____

© Houghton Mifflin Harcourt Publishing Company

Record Your Data

Draw and write to record what you observe.

_____

Draw Conclusions

What conclusions can you draw?

_____

_____

Ask More Questions

What other questions could you ask about the living things and objects observed around you?

_____

_____

© Houghton Mifflin Harcourt Publishing Company

TEKS **1.2C** collect data and make obervations using simple equipment ... **1.4A** collect, record, and compare information using tools ... **1.4B** measure and compare organisms and objects using non-standard units

Essential Question

What Are Science Tools?

🧠 Engage Your Brain!

Find the answer to the question in the lesson.

Which science tool would help this girl measure around the ball?

a _____

Active Reading

Lesson Vocabulary

1. Preview the lesson.
2. Write the 2 vocabulary terms here.

_____   _____

© Houghton Mifflin Harcourt Publishing Company

Inquiry Flipchart   p. 7 — It's Time to Measure/Balancing Act
pp. 8–9 — Science Tools Activities

Tools to Explore

You can use science tools to learn about the world around you. People use **science tools** to find out about things. Science tools help you collect, record, and compare information.

A hand lens is a science tool. It helps you observe small things. You could not see these things as well with just your eyes.

Active Reading

Find the sentence that tells about **science tools**. Draw a line under the sentence.

These children are using a hand lens to closely observe a flower.

© Houghton Mifflin Harcourt Publishing Company

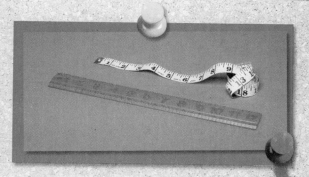

Ruler and Tape Measure

A ruler measures how long things are. A tape measure measures around things.

Measuring Cup

A measuring cup measures liquids.

Tools for Measuring

▶ **Read the labels. Circle the names of tools you use to measure.**

Balance

A balance compares how heavy things are.

Thermometer

A **thermometer** measures temperature. It tells how hot and cold things are.

© Houghton Mifflin Harcourt Publishing Company

Let's Measure!

You can measure objects in different ways. One way is to use another object such as a paper clip. Paper clips can help you collect and compare measurements.

You can also measure an object by using science tools. Many science tools have two kinds of units on them.

Active Reading

The main idea is the most important idea about something. Draw two lines under the main idea.

paper clips

© Houghton Mifflin Harcourt Publishing Company

Tools and Measurements

Tool	Unit of Measurement	
measuring cup	ounce	milliliter
ruler	inch	centimeter
tape measure	inch	centimeter
thermometer	degree Fahrenheit	degree Celsius

▶ **Look at the three pictures. Record the measurement on the line paired with each picture.**

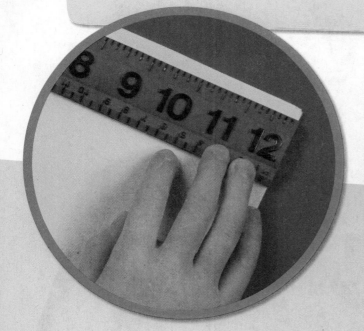

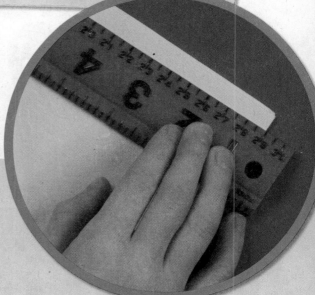

_____ inches

_____ centimeters

© Houghton Mifflin Harcourt Publishing Company

Measuring Up

Why should we use science tools to measure? What would happen if we used different things to measure the same object? We might get different measurements.

This girl is using her shoes to measure the rug.

© Houghton Mifflin Harcourt Publishing Company

Do the Math!

Measure Length

Measure how long a bookcase is. Use a small shoe, a large shoe, and a ruler or a tape measure. The ruler or tape measure should have units in centimeters and inches on it.

How long is the bookcase when you measure

1. with a small shoe?

   about _____ small shoes long

2. with a big shoe?

   about _____ big shoes long

3. with a ruler or a tape measure?

   about _____ centimeters long

   about _____ inches long

Compare all four measurements. Why should you use a ruler or a tape measure to measure the bookcase?

_____

_____

_____

_____

© Houghton Mifflin Harcourt Publishing Company

Sum It Up!

① Choose It!

Which tool is <u>not</u> used to measure? Mark an X on it.

② Circle It!

Which tool helps you observe small things? Circle it.

③ Match It!

Draw a line to match the tool with the kind of unit found on it.

thermometer	centimeter
ruler	degree Celsius
measuring cup	milliliter

© Houghton Mifflin Harcourt Publishing Company

Name _____

Word Play

Draw a line to the science tool whose name completes the sentence.

1. Measure temperature with a _____.

2. Measure water with a _____.

3. Observe an ant with a _____.

4. Compare how heavy with a _____.

5. Measure length with a _____.

© Houghton Mifflin Harcourt Publishing Company

Measure each object using paper clips. Then use a science tool to measure each object in centimeters and inches. Record your answers. Compare your measurements.

_____ paper clips _____ centimeters _____ inches

_____ paper clips _____ centimeters _____ inches

Which science tool did you use to measure the objects the second time?

_____

Family Members: Discuss with your child kinds of science tools. Go on a hunt together to find out how science tools are used in your home.

Take It Home!

© Houghton Mifflin Harcourt Publishing Company

Lesson **6**

Essential Question

How Do Scientists Work?

Engage Your Brain!

Find the answer to the question in the lesson.

How do you paint a rainbow using only three colors of paint?

You can mix

_____

Active Reading

Lesson Vocabulary

1 Preview the lesson.

2 Write the vocabulary term here.

_____

© Houghton Mifflin Harcourt Publishing Company

Think Like a Scientist

Scientists plan an investigation when they want to learn more. An **investigation** is a test scientists do. There are different plans for investigations. Here is one plan.

Observe

First, observe something. Ask a question about it.

Active Reading

Clue words can help you find the order of things. **First** is a clue word. Draw a box around this clue word.

What would happen if we mixed yellow paint and blue paint?

© Houghton Mifflin Harcourt Publishing Company

Hypothesize and Make a Plan

Next, make a hypothesis. State something you can test. Plan a fair test to see whether you are correct.

My Hypothesis

Blue paint and yellow paint mix to make green.

My Plan

1. Put yellow paint on a plate.
2. Put blue paint on a plate.
3. Mix the paints.

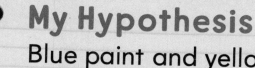

▶ Do you think yellow paint and blue paint mix to make green? Circle your answer.

Yes   No

© Houghton Mifflin Harcourt Publishing Company

Conduct the Test

Do the test. Follow the steps of your plan. Observe what happens.

Active Reading

The main idea is the most important idea about something. Draw two lines under the main idea.

We can mix the paints to see what happens.

© Houghton Mifflin Harcourt Publishing Company

Draw Conclusions

Draw conclusions from your test. What did you learn? Compare your results with your classmates' results. Use information you have collected to explain your results.

What would happen if you did the test again? How do you know?

If we do the test again, yellow paint and blue paint will still make green.

▶ Circle the color that yellow and blue make when you mix them.

© Houghton Mifflin Harcourt Publishing Company

Record What You Observe

Scientists record what they learn from an investigation. You can keep a record in a science notebook. You can draw pictures. You can write. You can also use numbers.

Active Reading

A detail is a fact about a main idea. Draw one line under a detail. Draw an arrow to the main idea it tells about.

© Houghton Mifflin Harcourt Publishing Company

Communicate

You can share what you have observed and learned with others. Writing, drawing, and speaking are ways to communicate.

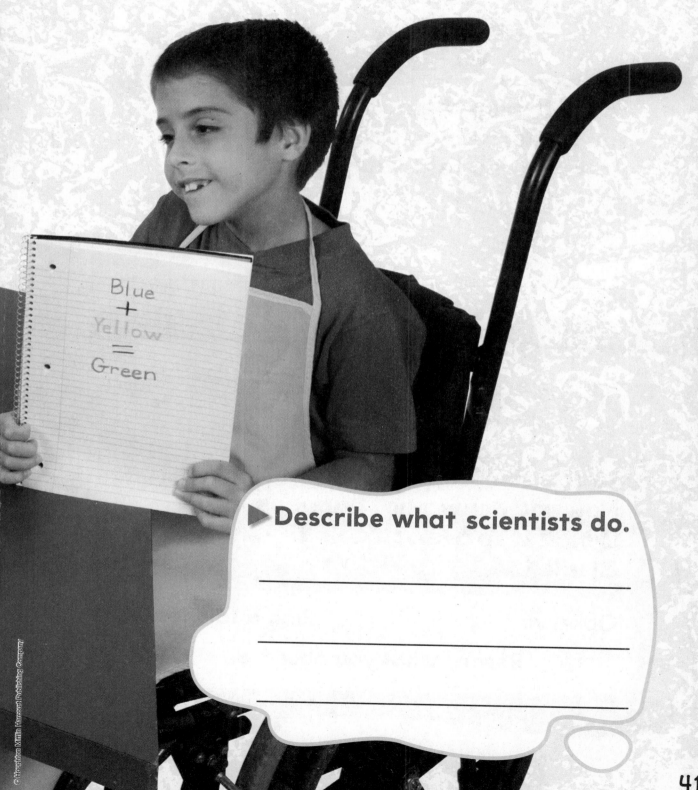

Blue
+
Yellow
=
Green

▶ **Describe what scientists do.**

_____

_____

_____

© Houghton Mifflin Harcourt Publishing Company

① Write It!

You have a  and a ☐ .
You will drop them.
You think the block will fall faster.
How can you test your idea?

_____

_____

② Circle It!

You do the steps in an investigation.
Now you draw what happens.
Which step are you doing?
Circle it.

Observe.   Plan a fair test.

Record what you observe.

© Houghton Mifflin Harcourt Publishing Company

Name _____

Word Play

Unscramble the word to complete each sentence. Use these words if you need help.

observe   hypothesize   investigation   record

ntiovetigansi

1. To learn more about something, you do an _____.

eyhtpoheszi

2. When you make a statement you can test, you _____.

dreorc

3. After you do a test, you should _____ your results.

beosver

4. When you look at something closely, you _____ it.

© Houghton Mifflin Harcourt Publishing Company

Apply Concepts

Can air move a penny and a feather? Describe what a scientist does. Tell how a scientist might investigate. Write a number from 1 to 5 to show the order.

_____ Write a plan.

_____ Ask a question—
Can air move a penny and a feather?

_____ Record what you observe.

_____ Share your results.

_____ Follow your plan.

Family Members: Ask your child to tell you about the steps of an investigation. Then plan and conduct an investigation you and your child can try at home.

Take It Home!

© Houghton Mifflin Harcourt Publishing Company

Learn About...
Mary Anderson

In 1902, Mary Anderson observed something. In bad weather, drivers had trouble seeing. They had to drive with the window open. Or they had to get out to clean off the windshield. Anderson got an idea. She invented the windshield wiper.

Drivers could use it from inside their vehicle. They could see the road and stay warm and dry.

Fun Fact

By the 1920s all cars had windshield wipers.

© Houghton Mifflin Harcourt Publishing Company   (bkgd) ©Comstock/Getty Images; (br) ©SSPL via Getty Images

This Leads to That

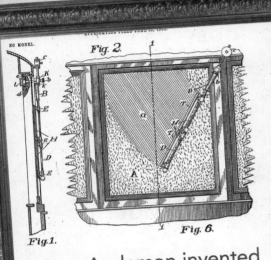

Mary Anderson invented the first windshield wiper. This shows an early drawing.

Robert Kearns invented a windshield wiper that went on and off as needed.

▶ **How does Mary Anderson's invention help people today?**

_____

_____

_____

© Houghton Mifflin Harcourt Publishing Company   (bkcd) ©Bettmann/Corbis (t) ©USPTO (tl) ©Richard Nowitz/Getty Images (photo frames) ©Getty Images/PhotoDisc

Vocabulary Review
Use the terms in the box to complete the sentences.

> inquiry skills
> investigation
> senses

1. You learn about the world by using your _____.

TEKS 1.3C
2. To find out information, scientists use _____.

TEKS 1.2B, 1.3C
3. To learn more, scientists plan an _____.

Science Concepts
Fill in the letter of the choice that best answers the question.

4. What can you learn from listening to music?
   - Ⓐ how it feels
   - Ⓑ how it looks
   - Ⓒ how it sounds

TEKS 1.4A
5. Which science tool can Sandra use to collect and compare air temperatures?
   - Ⓐ balance
   - Ⓑ measuring cup
   - Ⓒ thermometer

© Houghton Mifflin Harcourt Publishing Company

6. What question is the boy trying to answer about the flower?

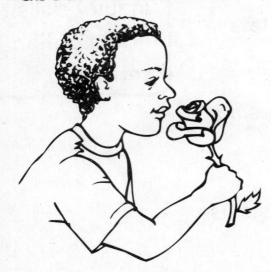

Ⓐ Are the flower petals soft or hard?

Ⓑ How does the flower smell?

Ⓒ Does the flower stem make a sound if it breaks?

7. A scientist does a fair test and writes about the results. What is the scientist doing?

Ⓐ classifying

Ⓑ communicating

Ⓒ measuring

8. You have two toy cars. You want to compare which is heavier. Which science tool will you use?

Ⓐ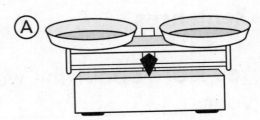

Ⓑ

Ⓒ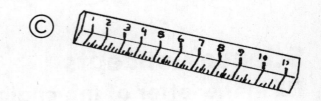

© Houghton Mifflin Harcourt Publishing Company

9. Pablo uses a hand lens to collect information about a plant. What does he observe?

Ⓐ the weight of the plant

Ⓑ the height of the plant

Ⓒ how the plant looks up close

10. Which step in an investigation is shown?

Ⓐ doing a test

Ⓑ drawing a conclusion

Ⓒ recording results

11. Alma does an investigation to find out how a bean plant grows. What can she do to communicate her results?

Ⓐ She can draw a picture of the bean plant each day.

Ⓑ She can ask a question about whether the plant needs water to grow.

Ⓒ She can repeat the investigation.

12. You are doing an investigation about different soils. What question could you use your sense of sight to answer?

Ⓐ How are the textures of the soils different?

Ⓑ How are the colors of the soils different?

Ⓒ How are the smells of the soils different?

© Houghton Mifflin Harcourt Publishing Company

Inquiry and the Big Idea
Write the answers to these questions.

13. Look at this picture.

a. What sense is the girl using?

_____

b. What can she learn by petting the dog?

_____

TEKS 1.2B

14. You want to plan and conduct an investigation about how fast two toy cars roll. Your hypothesis is that a metal car rolls faster than a wooden car. What steps would you follow to test your hypothesis?

_____

_____

_____

© Houghton Mifflin Harcourt Publishing Company

UNIT 2
Technology All Around Us

© Houghton Mifflin Harcourt Publishing Company (bkgd) ©Jeff Greenberg/Alamy; (border) ©NDisc/Age Fotostock

Big Idea

Engineers use a process to design and build something new. They use many different kinds of materials.

TEKS 1.1C, 1.2A, 1.2B, 1.2D, 1.3A, 1.3C, 1.5A

children's playground

I Wonder How

An engineer planned a design for this playground. How?
Turn the page to find out.

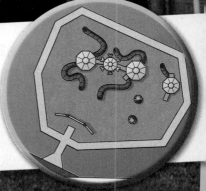

Here's How An engineer drew ideas on a plan. The plan had many fun things for kids.

In this unit, you will explore this Big Idea, the Essential Questions, and the Investigations on the Inquiry Flipchart.

Levels of Inquiry Key ▨ DIRECTED ▧ GUIDED ▨ INDEPENDENT

Track Your Progress

Big Idea Engineers use a process to design and build something new. They use many different kinds of materials.

Essential Questions

Lesson 1 How Do Engineers Work? 53
Inquiry Flipchart p. 11—Don't Crack Up!/Make It Fly!

Inquiry Lesson 2 How Can We Solve a Problem? 65
Inquiry Flipchart p. 12—How Can We Solve a Problem?

Lesson 3 What Materials Make Up Objects? 67
Inquiry Flipchart p. 13—Build It!/Materials Mission

Inquiry Lesson 4 How Can Materials Be Sorted? 79
Inquiry Flipchart p. 14—How Can Materials Be Sorted?

People in Science: Dr. Eugene Tsui 81

Unit 2 Review 83

Now I Get the Big Idea!

Science Notebook

Before you begin each lesson, be sure to write your thoughts about the Essential Question.

© Houghton Mifflin Harcourt Publishing Company (bkgd) ©Jeff Greenberg/Alamy; (border) ©Xfiber/Age Fotostock

Essential Question

How Do Engineers Work?

Engage Your Brain!

Find the answer to the question in the lesson.

How do you scratch an itch you can not reach?

You can

_____

_____ .

Active Reading

Lesson Vocabulary

1 Preview the lesson.

2 Write the 2 vocabulary terms here.

_____   _____

© Houghton Mifflin Harcourt Publishing Company   ©Pat McKillen/Alamy Images

Problem Solvers

An **engineer** is a person who uses math and science to solve everyday problems. Engineers work on many kinds of problems. Some engineers design robots. Others plan roads. Some design cars.

Active Reading

A detail is a fact about a main idea. Draw one line under a detail. Draw an arrow to the main idea it tells about.

► Circle the names of three kinds of engineers.

robotics engineer

© Houghton Mifflin Harcourt Publishing Company   ©George Steinmetz/Corbis

Engineers use a design process to solve problems. A **design process** is a plan with steps that help engineers find good solutions.

The Design Process

1. Find a Problem
2. Plan and Build
3. Test and Improve
4. Redesign
5. Communicate

mechanical engineer

civil engineer

© Houghton Mifflin Harcourt Publishing Company (bkgd) ©George Steinmetz/Corbis; (t) ©Radius Images/Alamy Images; (br) ©Tim Pannell/Corbis

The Design Process

1 **Find a Problem**

Jack has an itch he can not reach. How can he scratch it? The steps of this design process show Jack what to do.

Jack identifies his problem. He needs to find a way to scratch his back. He brainstorms ways to solve his problem.

Jack tries to scratch his back.

▶ **Identify and explain Jack's problem.**

_____

_____

© Houghton Mifflin Harcourt Publishing Company

Jack gets out his science notebook.
He wants to come up with a solution. Jack
records what he does to solve his problem:

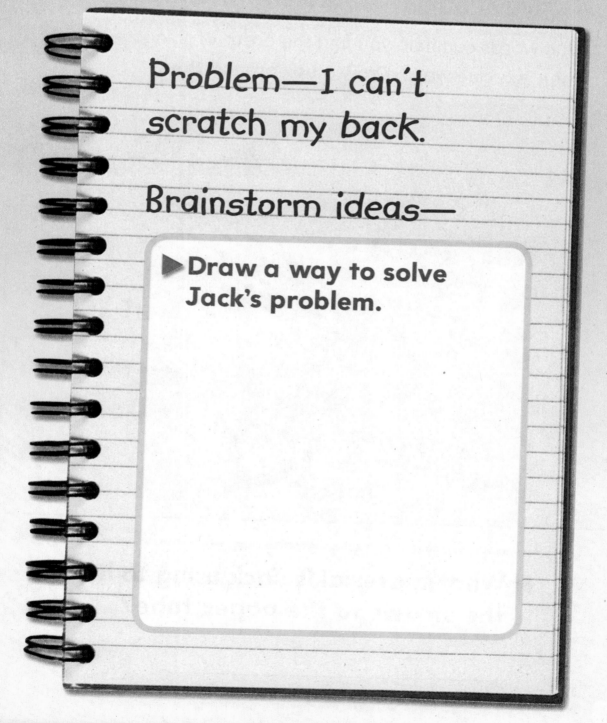

Problem—I can't
scratch my back.

Brainstorm ideas—

▶ **Draw a way to solve
Jack's problem.**

© Houghton Mifflin Harcourt Publishing Company

Then Jack chooses a solution to try. He makes a plan. Jack draws and labels his plan. He chooses the best materials to use.

Active Reading

Clue words can help you find the order of things. **Then** is a clue word. Draw a box around **then**.

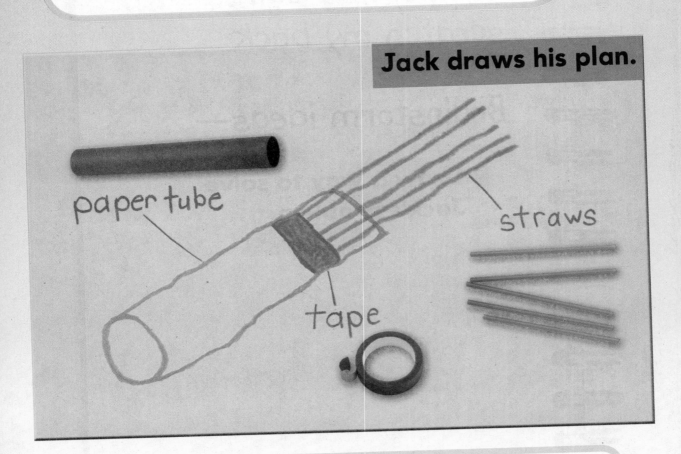

Jack draws his plan.

paper tube

straws

tape

▶ **What material is Jack using to hold the straws to the paper tube?**

_____

© Houghton Mifflin Harcourt Publishing Company

Jack builds his back scratcher.
He uses the materials he chose and the
plan he made.

Jack makes his
back scratcher.

© Houghton Mifflin Harcourt Publishing Company

Jack tests the back scratcher with a friend. They try the back scratcher to see whether it works. Does the back scratcher solve the problem?

▶ **Write a way to improve the design of the back scratcher.**

_____

_____

Jack and a friend test the back scratcher.

© Houghton Mifflin Harcourt Publishing Company

4 Redesign

Jack thinks of a way to redesign his back scratcher. He adds notes about how to make it better.

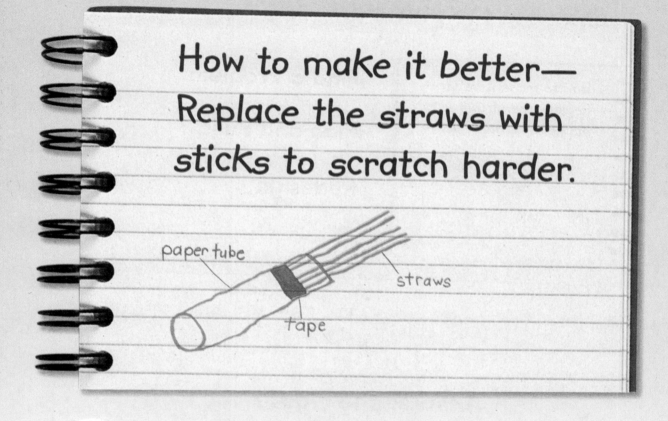

How to make it better—
Replace the straws with sticks to scratch harder.

paper tube

straws

tape

5 Communicate

Jack writes and draws to show what happened. He can share what he learned with others.

▶ **Which material is Jack using to make his design better? Circle the word.**

© Houghton Mifflin Harcourt Publishing Company

Sum It Up!

1 Circle It!

Circle the step of the design process shown in the picture.

How to make it better—
Replace the straws with
sticks to scratch harder.

paper tube

straws

tape

Find a Problem

Plan and Build

Redesign

2 Solve It!

Answer the riddle.

I solve problems using
science and math.
The design process leads
me along the right path.

Who am I?

_____

© Houghton Mifflin Harcourt Publishing Company

Name _____

Word Play

Write a label for each picture.

| choose materials | build | engineer | test |

_____   _____

_____   _____

© Houghton Mifflin Harcourt Publishing Company

Write numbers to put the steps of the design process in order. The first one is done for you.

The Design Process

_____ Test and Improve

____1____ Find a Problem

_____ Communicate

_____ Redesign

_____ Plan and Build

© Houghton Mifflin Harcourt Publishing Company

Take It Home!

Family Members: Help your child identify and explain a problem at home, such as a messy "junk drawer." Have your child come up with a solution using the design process.

TEKS **1.2A** ask questions about organisms, objects, and events observed in the natural world **1.2D** record and organize data using pictures, numbers, a words **1.3A** identify and explain a probl such as finding a home for a classroom p and propose a solution in his/her own wo

Name _____

Essential Question

How Can We Solve a Problem?

Set a Purpose

Identify and explain the problem.

_____

_____

Think About the Procedure

❶ What steps will you follow to build the home?

_____

_____

❷ How will you know that your design works?

_____

© Houghton Mifflin Harcourt Publishing Company

Record Your Data

Draw and label a picture of your solution.

Draw Conclusions

How did your solution work? How could you redesign the home to make it better?

_____

_____

Ask More Questions

What other questions could you ask about designing a solution to a problem?

_____

© Houghton Mifflin Harcourt Publishing Company

Essential Question

What Materials Make Up Objects?

🧠 Engage Your Brain!

Find the answer to the question in the lesson.

What could you make with this wood?

_____

Active Reading

Lesson Vocabulary

1 Preview the lesson.

2 Write the 3 vocabulary terms here.

_____   _____

_____

© Houghton Mifflin Harcourt Publishing Company (bkgd) ©Chris Howes/Wild Places Photography/Alamy Images

Play Your Part

Objects may be made of different parts. The parts go together to make the whole.

Look at this bicycle. It has wheels, a frame, and other parts. These parts go together to make a bicycle.

Active Reading

A detail is a fact about a main idea. Draw a line under a detail. Draw an arrow to the main idea it tells about.

_____

wheel
_____

_____

© Houghton Mifflin Harcourt Publishing Company   (bkgd) ©Don Mason/Blend Images/Corbis

Do the Math!

Solve a Problem

You are collecting bicycle tires to be used as mulch in the school's new playground. You collect 4 tires each day for 5 days. How many tires have you collected in all?

_____

▶ **Write labels for the parts of the bicycle.**

bicycle

6

A Material World

Look at this house. One part is brick. Another part is metal. Other parts are wood. The windows are glass.

Brick, metal, wood, and glass are materials. **Materials** are what objects are made of.

Active Reading

Find the sentence that tells the meaning of **materials**. Draw a line under the sentence.

brick

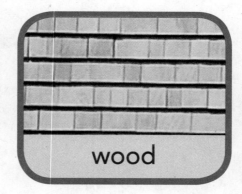

wood

glass

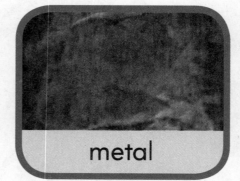

metal

▶Identify the materials on this house. Write a label for each part of the picture.

Made to Order

Materials are natural or human-made. **Natural** materials are found in nature. For example, cotton is from a plant. Wood is from trees. Metal comes from rocks.

People make **human-made** materials such as plastics and nylon. Scientists first made them in a lab. Scientists changed petroleum into these new materials not found in nature.

trees

cotton

Crude Oil

petroleum

© Houghton Mifflin Harcourt Publishing Company (tr) ©Bob Gibbons/Photo Researchers, Inc.; (cl) ©Lance Nelson/Stock Photos/Corbis; (br) ©Paul Rapson/Photo Researchers Inc.

cotton shirt

wooden boat with nylon sail

Some objects are made of natural materials. Others are made of human-made materials. Some objects are made of both natural and human-made materials.

►**Classify objects by the materials from which they are made. Circle the object made from natural materials. Draw an X on the objects made from human-made materials.**

plastic toys

© Houghton Mifflin Harcourt Publishing Company (tl) ©Getty Images/Photodisc/C Squared Studios; (br) ©Martin Wierink/Alamy

Everyday Materials

What is made from cotton? Do you have a pair of jeans? Cotton jeans are made in factories. Here is how.

Active Reading

Things may happen in order. Draw a line under the step that happens first.

© Houghton Mifflin Harcourt Publishing Company (bkgd) ©Martin Barraud/Getty Images

1 Looms weave cotton into cloth.

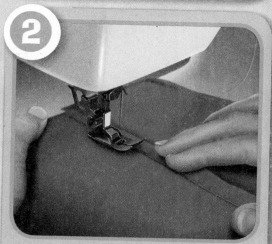

2 Workers use machines to cut and sew the cloth.

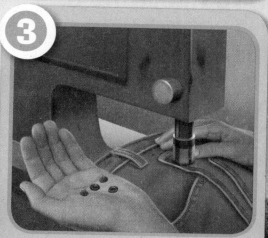

3 Workers use machines to put on metal rivets.

4 Now the jeans are ready to wear!

© Houghton Mifflin Harcourt Publishing Company · (t) ©Jose Luis Pelaez Inc./Getty Images; (bkgd) ©Martin Barraud/Getty Images

Sum It Up!

① Draw It!

Draw something made of glass on the house.

② Match It!

Identify the material each toy is made of. Draw a line from the word to the picture.

| human-made | natural | human-made and natural |

© Houghton Mifflin Harcourt Publishing Company (br) ©D. Hurst/Alamy Images

Name _____

Word Play

Color the letters to spell the vocabulary words.
Write the words to complete the sentences.

human-made   **materials**   **natural**

n	a	t	u	r	a	l	t	w	k
c	t	o	w	r	e	g	y	p	s
h	u	m	a	n	m	a	d	e	y
g	m	a	t	e	r	i	a	l	s
k	n	y	u	o	s	d	x	p	m

1. Objects are made of _____.

2. Materials made in a lab are _____.

3. Materials found in nature are _____.

© Houghton Mifflin Harcourt Publishing Company   (b) ©Terry Matthews/Alamy Images

Complete the chart. Identify and classify the materials each object is made from.

Materials Chart

Object	Material	Natural, human-made, or both
①	_____	_____
②	_____ _____	_____
③	_____	_____

Family Members: Play a game with your child to identify the parts and materials of objects around the home. Classify the materials as natural, human-made, or both.

Take It Home!

© Houghton Mifflin Harcourt Publishing Company (bl) ©D. Hurst/Alamy Images

Inquiry Flipchart p. 14

Lesson **4**

INQUIRY

TEKS **1.2A** ask questions about organisms, objects, and events observed the natural world **1.2B** plan and conduc simple descriptive investigations such as ways objects move **1.2D** record and organize data using pictures, numbers, a words **1.5A** classify objects by observabl properties of the materials from which th are made . . .

Name _____

Essential Question

How Can Materials Be Sorted?

Set a Purpose
Tell what you want to do.

_____

_____

Think About the Procedure
❶ What will you observe about the objects?

_____

_____

❷ How will you sort the objects?

_____

_____

© Houghton Mifflin Harcourt Publishing Company

Record Your Data

Classify the objects using the chart below. Draw or write to record how you grouped the objects.

Natural	Human-made	Both

Draw Conclusions

How could you tell what objects were made of?

_____

_____

Ask More Questions

What other questions could you ask about objects and materials?

_____

_____

© Houghton Mifflin Harcourt Publishing Company

Get to Know
Dr. Eugene Tsui

Dr. Eugene Tsui is an architect. This is a kind of engineer. An architect designs homes and other buildings.

Dr. Tsui studies forms in nature, such as sea shells. He bases his designs on what he learns. Dr. Tsui says that nature is our greatest teacher.

Fun Fact

Dr. Tsui also designs his own clothes.

© Houghton Mifflin Harcourt Publishing Company   (bkg) ©Stade Pres/Getty Images/PhotoDisc; (c) ©Eugene Tsui; (b) ©Eugene Tsui

Dr. Tsui's Designs

▶ Draw a line from each building to the natural form it is based on.

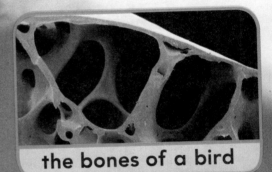

the bones of a bird

fish scales

dragonfly wings

▶ Think about a form from nature.
Use it to design your own building.

© Houghton Mifflin Harcourt Publishing Company   (bkgd) ©Siede Preis /(Getty Images/PhotoDisc; (tl, cl, bl) ©Eugene Tsui; (tr) ©Eye of Science/Photo Researchers, Inc; (cr) ©Yasufide Fumoto/Getty Images; (br) ©Dorling Kindersley/Getty Images

Vocabulary Review

Use the terms in the box to complete the sentences.

> engineer
> materials
> natural

1. An _____ might try to solve a problem such as how to build a better car.

TEKS 1.1C

2. Brick, metal, and wood are all different _____.

TEKS 1.1C

3. Cotton and wood are _____ things found in nature.

Science Concepts

Fill in the letter of the choice that best answers the question.

TEKS 1.1C, 1.5A

4. A cotton shirt has a metal zipper. How can you classify the materials that make up the shirt?

(A) natural

(B) human-made

(C) both natural and human-made

TEKS 1.3A

5. Yazan observes that the food in a bird feeder is hard for birds to get. What step of the design process has he just completed?

(A) Communicate

(B) Find a Problem

(C) Test and Improve

© Houghton Mifflin Harcourt Publishing Company

6. Cara is looking at two objects.

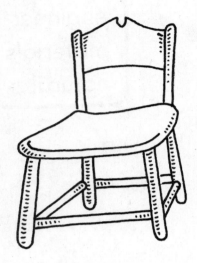

Which object is made from a human-made material?

Ⓐ the wooden chair

Ⓑ the plastic bucket

Ⓒ both are made from human-made materials

7. An engineer designs a bike that folds in half. What problem might she be trying to solve?

Ⓐ Bikes cannot fit in small spaces.

Ⓑ Bikes are hard to ride.

Ⓒ Bikes are too slow.

8. Which object is made from natural materials?

Ⓐ a nylon shirt

Ⓑ a plastic bottle

Ⓒ a wooden table

9. Raj's pencil stand falls over when it is full. How can he try to solve this problem?

Ⓐ He can throw the pencil stand away.

Ⓑ He can plan and build a better pencil stand.

Ⓒ He can find a different problem to solve.

© Houghton Mifflin Harcourt Publishing Company

10. A river is between two towns. People want to drive from one town to the other. Two engineers talk about the problem.

How do they plan to solve it?

Ⓐ build a tunnel under the river

Ⓑ build a bridge over the river

Ⓒ give boats to the people in the towns

11. You use the design process to design a sun hat. How can you communicate what you did?

Ⓐ Test that the hat blocks the sun.

Ⓑ Tell others how your design works.

Ⓒ Redesign the hat and make changes.

12. Which object is made of both natural materials and human-made materials?

Ⓐ a metal bucket with a wooden handle

Ⓑ a wooden door with a metal handle

Ⓒ a cotton bag with a plastic handle

© Houghton Mifflin Harcourt Publishing Company

Inquiry and the Big Idea
Write the answers to these questions.

TEKS 1.1C, 1.5A

13. Geeta sorted objects into these two groups.

Group 1	Group 2
wooden pencil	plastic toy
metal fork	nylon jacket

a. How did she classify the objects?

_____

_____

b. Name one thing that could be added to each group.

_____

TEKS 1.3A

14. Cold air is coming in under Michael's door. He wants to use the design process to find a solution.

a. What should Michael do first?

_____

b. Michael builds a tool. How can he test it?

_____

c. What should he do if the tool does not work?

_____

© Houghton Mifflin Harcourt Publishing Company

Matter

sandcastle

© Houghton Mifflin Harcourt Publishing Company (bkgd) ©Pete Gridley/Getty Images; (inset) ©Andrew Paterson/Alamy; (inset) ©Mimi Haddon/BrandXPictures/Getty Images; (border) ©NDisc/Age Fotostock

Big Idea

All objects are matter. Matter can change in different ways.

TEKS 1.2A, 1.2B, 1.2D, 1.3A, 1.3C, 1.5A, 1.5B

I Wonder Why

We use the words brown and rough to tell about this sandcastle. Why?

Turn the page to find out.

Here's Why <u>Brown</u> and <u>rough</u> are properties of the sandcastle. A property is one part of what something is like.

In this unit, you will explore this Big Idea, the Essential Questions, and the Investigations on the Inquiry Flipchart.

Levels of Inquiry Key ■ DIRECTED ■ GUIDED ■ INDEPENDENT

Track Your Progress

Big Idea All objects are matter. Matter can change in different ways.

Essential Questions

Lesson 1 What Can We Observe About Objects? 89
Inquiry Flipchart p. 15—Sort It Out!/What's the Weight?

🛈 **Careers in Science:** Polymer Scientist 101

Inquiry Lesson 2 How Can We Measure Temperature? . .103
Inquiry Flipchart p. 16—How Can We Measure Temperature?

Lesson 3 How Does Heating and Cooling Change Matter? 105
Inquiry Flipchart p. 17—Water to Gas/Water Changes

S.T.E.M. Engineering and Technology: Kitchen Technology 115
Inquiry Flipchart p. 18—Think About Process: Write a Recipe

Unit 3 Review 117

Now I Get the Big Idea!

Science Notebook

Before you begin each lesson, be sure to write your thoughts about the Essential Question.

© Houghton Mifflin Harcourt Publishing Company (bkgd) ©Peter Endley/Getty Images; (inset) ©Andrew Paterson/Alamy; (inset) ©Mimi Haddon/BrandXPictures/Getty Image; (border) ©NDisc/Age Fotostock

Lesson **1**

Essential Question

What Can We Observe About Objects?

Engage Your Brain!

Find the answer to the question in the lesson.

How are the blocks in this rabbit the same?

They are all

_____.

Active Reading

Lesson Vocabulary

❶ Preview the lesson.

❷ Write the 5 vocabulary terms here.

_____   _____

_____   _____

_____

© Houghton Mifflin Harcourt Publishing Company   (bkgd) ©John MacDougall/AFP/Getty Images

Why Matter Matters

Look around. What do you see? Are there trees, toys, or books? These things are matter. **Matter** is anything that takes up space. Even the air you breathe is matter!

Active Reading

The main idea is the most important idea about something. Draw two lines under the main idea.

© Houghton Mifflin Harcourt Publishing Company

Look at the ball, the clock, and the boy. Draw an X on each thing that is matter.

© Houghton Mifflin Harcourt Publishing Company

What's It Like?

A **property** of matter is one part of what something is like. Some properties are size, shape, color, and texture. **Texture** is what an object feels like.

Active Reading

Find the sentence that tells the meaning of **property**. Draw a line under the sentence.

Size

Big and **small** are words that tell about size.

Shape

Star and **heart** are words that tell about shape.

© Houghton Mifflin Harcourt Publishing Company. (t) ©Brand X Pictures/Getty Images; (b) ©Joanna McCarthy/Getty Images; (car) ©Shinypix/Alamy; (starfish) ©Doring Kindersley/Getty Images; (star) ©pixel shepherd/Alamy; (heart) ©Simone Brandt/Alamy

You can classify objects by the properties of the materials they are made from. When you classify, you put things that are alike in the same group.

▶ In each box, draw an X on the object that does not belong.

Color
Red and **blue** are words that tell about color.

Texture
Soft and **hard** are words that tell about texture.

© Houghton Mifflin Harcourt Publishing Company; (t) ©Brand X Pictures/Getty Images; (b) ©Joanna McCarthy/Getty Images; (crayon) ©Richard Heyes/Alamy; (teddy bear) ©Jon Helgason/Alamy; (panda) ©Ingram/Getty Images

Heavy or Light?

Some things you pick up feel light. Others feel heavy. **Weight** is the measure of how heavy an object feels. You can classify objects by their weight.

heavy

light

Do the Math!

Order by Weight

Order from light to heavy. Write 1 for lightest. Write 3 for heaviest.

paint

_____

paper clip

_____

marker

_____

94

© Houghton Mifflin Harcourt Publishing Company

Hot or Cold?

How hot is a pizza? How cold is an ice pop? You can find out by using temperature. **Temperature** is the measure of how hot or cold something is.

pizza

ice pop

hot cocoa

lemonade

▶ Draw something hot.

▶ Draw something cold.

© Houghton Mifflin Harcourt Publishing Company

Will It Sink or Will It Float?

Think about things in a tub or a pool. A sponge may stay on top of the water. A bar of soap may go to the bottom.

An object that floats stays on top of a liquid. An object that sinks falls to the bottom.

▶Circle what floats. Draw an X on what sinks.

© Houghton Mifflin Harcourt Publishing Company

The canoe with people is big and heavy.

Why does it float?

How Does That Boat Float?

Look at the clay boat and the clay ball. The ball sinks. The boat floats. Why? The ball and the boat have different shapes. The shape of the boat helps it float. Sometimes changing the shape of something makes it sink or float.

© Houghton Mifflin Harcourt Publishing Company ©Simon Marcus/Corbis

Sum It Up!

① Choose It!

Classify the objects. Circle each blue shape. Draw an X on each square. Underline each big circle.

② Mark It!

Draw an X on the small dog.

③ Write It!

Is this toy soft or hard?
Write the word.

_____

98

© Houghton Mifflin Harcourt Publishing Company (br) ©Ingram/Getty Images

Name _____

Word Play

Write the word from the box for each clue.

| property | weight | texture | temperature |

the measure of how hot or cold something is

___ ___(1)___ ___ ___(2)___ ___ ___ ___

the way something feels

(3)___ ___ ___(4)___ ___ ___ ___

the measure of how heavy something feels

___(5)___ ___ ___ ___ ___

a part of what something is like

___ ___ ___ ___ ___(6)___ ___

Solve the riddle. Write the circled letters in order on the lines below.

I am anything that takes up space.
What am I? ___ ___ ___ ___ ___ ___
              1   2   3   4   5   6

© Houghton Mifflin Harcourt Publishing Company

1 Classify these shapes by their properties. Draw each one in the diagram.

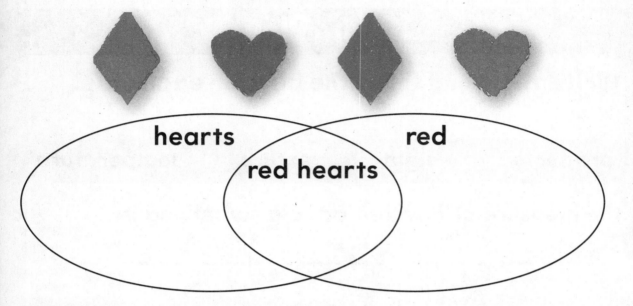

hearts   red

red hearts

2 Circle each thing that floats.

Draw an X on each thing that sinks.

3 Name or draw something hot. _____

Name or draw something cold. _____

Take It Home!

Family Members: Ask your child to tell you about the properties of matter. Point out objects at home. Have your child classify the objects by their properties.

© Houghton Mifflin Harcourt Publishing Company (bc) ©Corbis (br) ©D.Hurst/Alamy

Ask a Polymer Scientist

What are polymers?

Polymers are a kind of material. We can find some polymers, such as silk, in nature. Scientists make other polymers, such as plastics.

What does a polymer scientist do?

I work with different materials to make them better. Materials can cause problems. I try to solve the problems.

What is one problem that polymer scientists are working on?

Some polymers take years to break down. This makes a lot of garbage. Scientists want to make polymers that break down faster so there is less garbage.

Now It's Your Turn!

▶ **Describe what a polymer scientist does.**

_____

_____

_____

_____

© Houghton Mifflin Harcourt Publishing Company © Peter Ginter/Science Faction/Corbis

Polymer Play

▶ Think about what a polymer scientist studies. Make a list of polymers on the lines below.

rubber ball

foam peanuts

plastic toy

1 _____

2 _____

3 _____

4 _____

plastic bags

Fun Fact

A lobster's shell is a polymer.

© Houghton Mifflin Harcourt Publishing Company (rubber ball) ©John Wilkes Studio/Corbis; (foam peanuts) ©John Wilkes Studio/Corbis; (toy car) © D. Hurst/Alamy; (bags) ©Andy Crawford/Getty Images; (lobster) © Rainer Holz/Corbis

TEKS **1.2A** Ask questions about organisms, objects, and events observe the natural world **1.2B** plan and cond simple descriptive investigations such as ways objects move **1.2D** record an organize data using pictures, numbers, words **1.5B** predict and identify chang in materials caused by heating and cool such as ice melting, water freezing, and water evaporating

Lesson 2
INQUIRY

Name _____

Essential Question

How Can We Measure Temperature?

Set a Purpose
Tell what you will find out.

_____

Think About the Procedure
❶ How will you test whether light colors or dark colors warm up faster?

_____

_____

❷ How do you know which color warms up faster?

_____

_____

© Houghton Mifflin Harcourt Publishing Company

Record Your Data

In this chart, record the temperature at the beginning and the temperature after 30 minutes. Compare them.

Color	Beginning Temperature	Temperature After 30 Minutes
White		
Black		

Draw Conclusions

Do light colors or dark colors warm up faster?

_____

Ask More Questions

What other questions about temperature could you ask?

_____

_____

_____

© Houghton Mifflin Harcourt Publishing Company

TEKS **1.5B** predict and identify changes in materials caused by heating and cooling such as ice melting, water freezing, and water evaporating

Lesson **3**

Essential Question

How Does Heating and Cooling Change Matter?

Engage Your Brain!

Find the answer to the question in the lesson.

How does water turn to ice?

It _____.

Active Reading

Lesson Vocabulary

❶ Preview the lesson.

❷ Write the 4 vocabulary terms here.

_____   _____

_____   _____

© Houghton Mifflin Harcourt Publishing Company ©Richard Prudhomme/Demotix/Corbis

Freeze in Place

Cooling changes water. Taking away heat makes water freeze. **Freeze** means to change from a liquid to a solid. Water freezes into ice. Other liquids, such as juice, can freeze, too.

Active Reading

Find the sentence that tells the meaning of **freeze**. Draw a line under the sentence.

A lake can freeze into ice.

1

© Houghton Mifflin Harcourt Publishing Company ⦁ (t) ©Dennis Flaherty/Photo Researchers, Inc.

The water turns to ice. Ice is solid and cold.

Water is a liquid.
Water loses heat when it
goes into a cold place.

▶Identify what
happens to water
when it is cooled.

_____

© Houghton Mifflin Harcourt Publishing Company

Melt Away

Heat from the sun warms ice. Then what? The ice melts! **Melt** means to change from a solid to a liquid. Ice melts and changes into water. Other solids melt when heated, too.

1

The ice is still frozen.

2

Heat melts the ice.

© Houghton Mifflin Harcourt Publishing Company

1 What happens when crayons are left out in the sun?

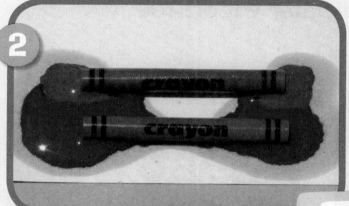

2 Heat from the sun melts them. They become a liquid.

1

2 ▶ What will happen to ice cream left in the sun? Draw to predict it!

© Houghton Mifflin Harcourt Publishing Company

Up in the Air

Water dries. Where does it go? It evaporates. **Evaporate** means to change from a liquid to a gas. The more heat you add, the faster the water will evaporate. Water in the air is called water vapor. You can not see it.

1

The puddle is liquid.

2

Heat turns the puddle into a gas.

▶ **Predict what will happen to the water in these footprints in the sun.**

_____

_____

© Houghton Mifflin Harcourt Publishing Company   (b) ©Chris Hackett/Tetra Images/Alamy Images

Cool It!

What happens when water vapor cools? Cooling makes water vapor condense into water. **Condense** means to change from a gas to a liquid.

Active Reading

An effect tells what happens. Draw two lines under an effect.

Water vapor condenses into water on the mirror.

1

2

© Houghton Mifflin Harcourt Publishing Company

Sum It Up!

1 Mark It!

Predict which one will evaporate faster. Mark it with an X.

2 Circle It!

Identify which one is frozen. Circle it.

3 Draw It!

Draw an object before and after it melts.

Before	After

© Houghton Mifflin Harcourt Publishing Company

Name _____

Word Play

Write the word that describes the underlined words in each sentence.

| melt | freeze | evaporate | condense |

1. Heating makes <u>a solid turn into a liquid</u>. _____

2. Heating makes <u>a liquid turn into a gas</u>. _____

3. Cooling makes <u>a liquid turn into a solid</u>. _____

4. Cooling makes <u>a gas turn into a liquid</u>. _____

© Houghton Mifflin Harcourt Publishing Company

Apply Concepts

Identify the change that happened.
Write the missing word for each effect.

Cause   **Effect**

| Gas is cooled. | It _____ into a liquid. |

| Water is heated. | It _____ into a gas. |

| Water is cooled. | It _____ into a solid. |

| Ice is heated. | It _____ into water. |

Take It Home!

Family Members: Work with your child to identify foods, liquids, and other materials in your home that can freeze, melt, and evaporate.

© Houghton Mifflin Harcourt Publishing Company

TEKS 1.3A identify and explain a problem such as finding a home for a classroom pet and propose a solution in his/her own words

S.T.E.M.
Engineering and Technology

Kitchen Technology
Cooking Tools

The tools you use to cook are technology. They are designed to help you in the kitchen! A recipe tells you how to make food. A spoon helps you measure. An oven helps you bake.

Whole Wheat Chocolate Chip Cookies
1 egg
1 teaspoon vanilla
1 teaspoon baking soda
2 cups whole wheat flour

Measuring cups and spoons have units that help you measure correctly.

A timer tells you when something has finished baking.

© Houghton Mifflin Harcourt Publishing Company (b) ©Sean Justice/Getty Images; (bc) ©Getty Images; (t) ©Corbis

Make Do

Write a solution for each problem.

1 You are baking muffins. The timer on your oven is broken! How else could you measure how long to bake the muffins?

_____

_____

2 You need 3 cups of flour for a recipe. You only have a 1-cup measuring cup. How could you use it to measure the flour?

_____

_____

Build On It!

Write about your favorite sandwich recipe. Complete **Think About Process: Write a Recipe** on the Inquiry Flipchart.

© Houghton Mifflin Harcourt Publishing Company (t) Cimage Source/Getty

Name _____

Vocabulary Review

Use the terms in the box to complete the sentences.

condense
property
texture

TEKS 1.5A

1. One part of what something is like is a _____.

TEKS 1.5A

2. You can classify an object by its _____, or how hard or soft it is.

TEKS 1.5B

3. To _____ is to cool and change from a gas to a liquid.

Science Concepts

Fill in the letter of the choice that best answers the question.

TEKS 1.5A

4. How is all matter the **same**?

   Ⓐ All matter has the same shape.

   Ⓑ All matter takes up space.

   Ⓒ All matter is made from natural materials.

TEKS 1.2B, 1.5A

5. John is conducting an investigation. He picks up two objects. One is heavier than the other. How can he classify the objects?

   Ⓐ by color

   Ⓑ by shape

   Ⓒ by weight

© Houghton Mifflin Harcourt Publishing Company

6. The boy puts the tray in a cold place. What does he predict will happen to the water in the tray?

Ⓐ It will evaporate.
Ⓑ It will freeze.
Ⓒ It will melt.

7. How are these rocks classified?

Ⓐ by color
Ⓑ by shape
Ⓒ by size

8. Use the cups of water and the thermometers to compare temperatures. Which cup has the hottest water?

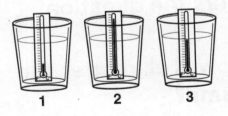

1   2   3

Ⓐ cup 1
Ⓑ cup 2
Ⓒ cup 3

© Houghton Mifflin Harcourt Publishing Company

TEKS 1.5B

9. How is the ice cube changing? Identify it.

Ⓐ It is freezing.
Ⓑ It is melting.
Ⓒ It is condensing.

TEKS 1.5A

10. You observe a group of square blocks and a group of round blocks. How are they classified?
Ⓐ by color
Ⓑ by size
Ⓒ by shape

TEKS 1.2B, 1.4A

11. Jin measures the temperature at different times. Compare them. At which time is it coldest?

Time of Day	Temperature
morning	32 °F
afternoon	42 °F
night	25 °F

Ⓐ morning
Ⓑ afternoon
Ⓒ night

TEKS 1.5B

12. A lake freezes into ice. What can you tell about the temperature where the lake is?
Ⓐ It is cold.
Ⓑ It is hot.
Ⓒ It is warm.

© Houghton Mifflin Harcourt Publishing Company

Inquiry and the Big Idea

Write the answers to these questions.

TEKS 1.2B, 1.4A, 1.5B

13. These two cups started with water at 25 °C.

They both stayed in the sun for 30 minutes.

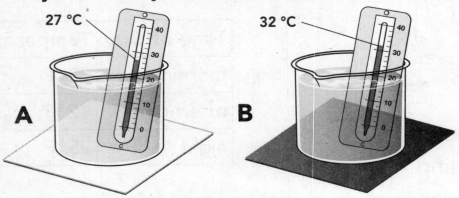

27 °C   A

32 °C   B

a. Identify the cup of water that heated up more. How can you tell?

_____

b. Why did this happen?

_____

_____

TEKS 1.5B

14. The sun shines on a puddle. Predict how the puddle will change. Explain.

_____

_____

_____

© Houghton Mifflin Harcourt Publishing Company

Forces and Energy

© Houghton Mifflin Harcourt Publishing Company

Big Idea

Forces change the way objects move. Magnets attract some objects and repel others. Energy can cause matter to move or change.

TEKS 1.2A, 1.2B, 1.2D, 1.3A, 1.3C, 1.6A, 1.6B, 1.6C, 1.6D

miniature golf course

I Wonder Why

The ball moves when you hit it. Why?
Turn the page to find out.

Here's Why A force pushes the ball and makes it move to a new location. In this unit, you will explore this Big Idea, the Essential Questions, and the Investigations on the Inquiry Flipchart.

Levels of Inquiry Key ▬ DIRECTED ▬ GUIDED ▬ INDEPENDENT

Track Your Progress

Big Idea Forces change the way objects move. Magnets attract some objects and repel others. Energy can cause matter to move or change.

Essential Questions

Lesson 1 How Do We Use Energy? 123
Inquiry Flipchart p. 19—Making Toast/My Energy Survey

Lesson 2 How Do Magnets Move Objects? 135
Inquiry Flipchart p. 20— Push and Pull/Which Magnet Will Win?

Lesson 3 How Do Objects Move? 145
Inquiry Flipchart p. 21—Marble Race/Testing Toys

People in Science: Isaac Newton 153

Inquiry Lesson 4 How Can We Move a Ball? 155
Inquiry Flipchart p. 22—How Can We Move a Ball?

**Lesson 5 How Can We Change the Way
Objects Move?** 157
Inquiry Flipchart p. 23—Changing Motion/Changing Location

S.T.E.M. Engineering and Technology: Fly to the Sky . . . 169
Inquiry Flipchart p. 24—Build It: Paper Airplanes

Unit 4 Review 171

Now I Get the Big Idea!

Science Notebook
Before you begin each lesson, be sure to write your thoughts about the Essential Question.

© Houghton Mifflin Harcourt Publishing Company

TEKS **1.6A** identify and discuss how different forms of energy such as light, heat, and sound are important to everyday life

Lesson **1**

Essential Question

How Do We Use Energy?

Engage Your Brain!

Find the answer to the question in the lesson.

What kind of energy lets us see the truck at night?

_____ energy

Active Reading

Lesson Vocabulary

1 Preview the lesson.

2 Write the 5 vocabulary terms here.

_____   _____   _____

_____   _____

© Houghton Mifflin Harcourt Publishing Company (b) ©Oliver Niclls/The Image Bank/Getty Images

Full of Energy

We use energy every day. **Energy** is something that can cause matter to move or change. Where do you see energy at work in this city?

Active Reading

Find the sentence that tells the meaning of **energy**. Draw a line under the sentence.

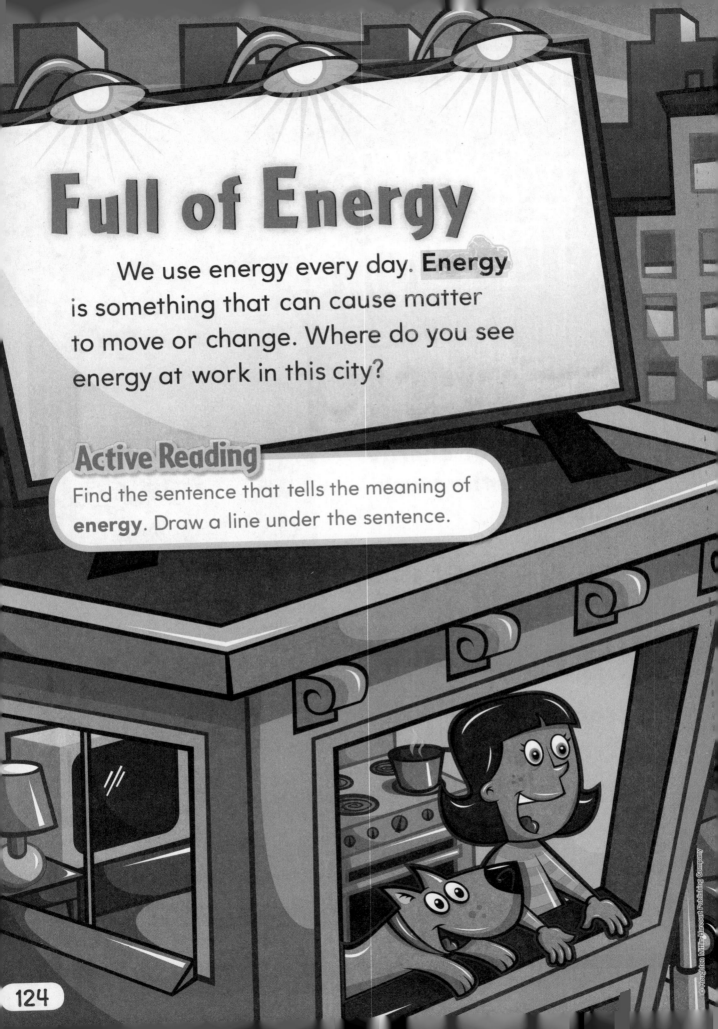

© Houghton Mifflin Harcourt Publishing Company

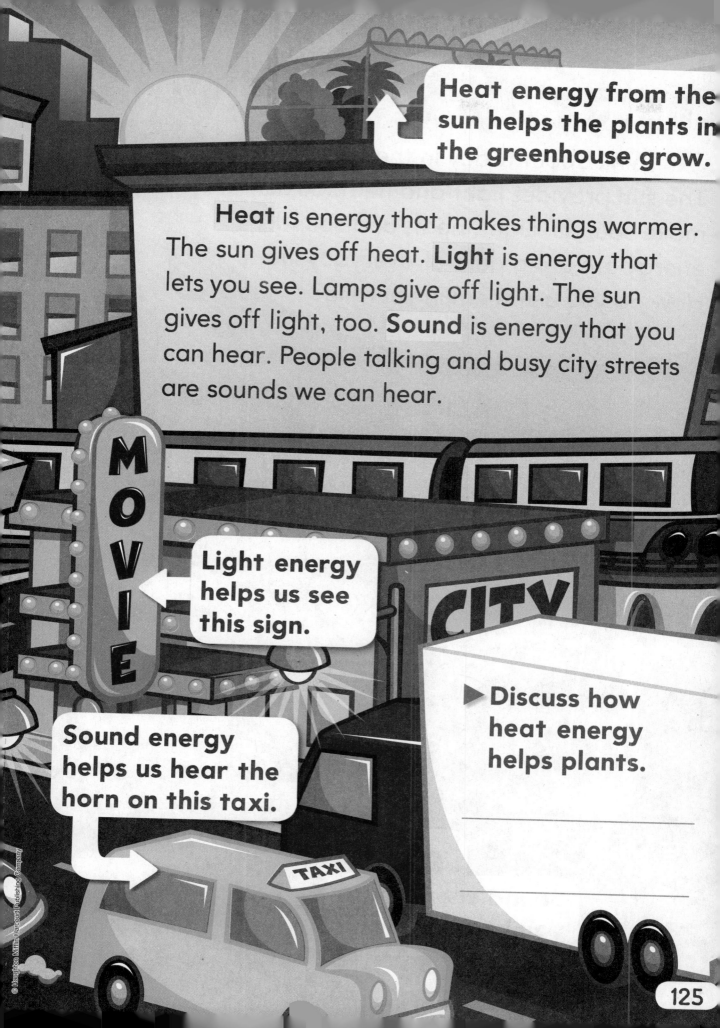

Heat energy from the sun helps the plants in the greenhouse grow.

Heat is energy that makes things warmer. The sun gives off heat. **Light** is energy that lets you see. Lamps give off light. The sun gives off light, too. **Sound** is energy that you can hear. People talking and busy city streets are sounds we can hear.

Light energy helps us see this sign.

Sound energy helps us hear the horn on this taxi.

▶ Discuss how heat energy helps plants.

© Houghton Mifflin Harcourt Publishing Company

Energy All Around

Think about a day in the park. The sun provides light and heat. Birds make sounds. Light, heat, and sound energy are a big part of everyday life. How do you use them in your life?

Sound energy lets you hear music.

© Houghton Mifflin Harcourt Publishing Company

Name three kinds of energy. Identify and discuss how they are important to everyday life.

_____

_____

_____

Light energy lets you see the park and the food stand when it gets dark.

HOT DOGS

FOOD

FRESH

Heat energy helps us cook food.

© Houghton Mifflin Harcourt Publishing Company

Electricity at Home

Things like toasters, lamps, and radios change electricity into heat, light, and sound. **Electricity** is energy that provides power for many things we use each day.

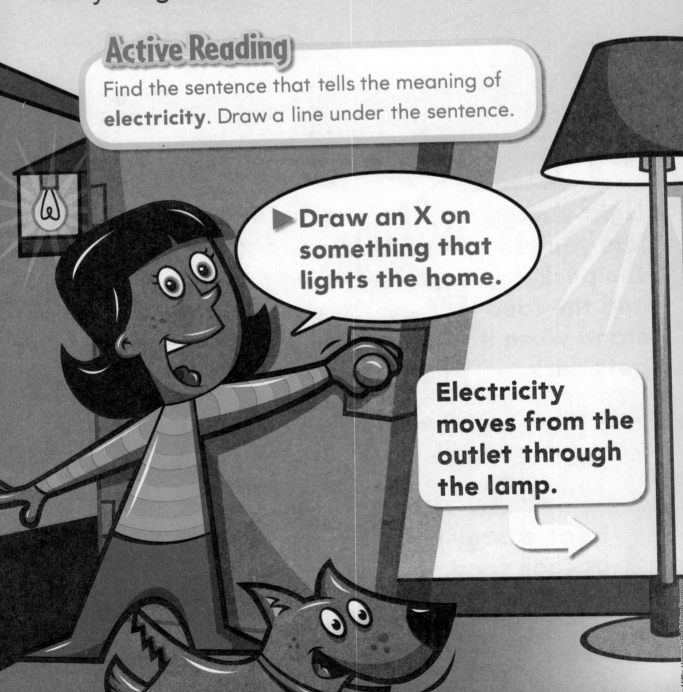

Active Reading

Find the sentence that tells the meaning of **electricity**. Draw a line under the sentence.

▶ Draw an X on something that lights the home.

Electricity moves from the outlet through the lamp.

© Houghton Mifflin Harcourt Publishing Company

© Houghton Mifflin Harcourt Publishing Company

Kinds of Energy

Many kinds of energy provide power for the things we use each day. You can see some of these kinds of energy on these pages. People use most of them to produce electricity.

This dam uses water to produce electricity.

▶ Identify two kinds of energy you see on these pages.

_____

_____

© Houghton Mifflin Harcourt Publishing Company

Wind farms collect energy from the wind.

Solar panels collect energy from the sun.

Do the Math!
Solve a Problem

Read the word problem. Answer the question.

There are two solar panels on each house. How many solar panels are there on four houses?

_____

© Houghton Mifflin Harcourt Publishing Company (bkgd) ©Klaus Hackenberg/Corbis; (t) ©Harmund Koch/Corbis; (b) ©Dietrich Rose/Corbis

Sum It Up!

① Label It!

Look at the pictures. Identify the kind of energy you see. Label it.

_____   _____   _____

② Choose It!

Circle the sentence that tells about light energy.

We use it to cook food.

It lets us see.

It is energy we can hear.

③ Draw It!

Draw a way that you use electricity.

© Houghton Mifflin Harcourt Publishing Company

Name _____

Word Play

Write a word for each clue. Find each word in the word search. Then answer the question.

1. something that can make matter move or change ___ ___ ___ ___ ___ ___

2. energy that lets us see ___ ___ ___ ___ ___

3. energy we can hear ___ ___ ___ ___ ___

4. energy that makes things warmer ___ ___ ___ ___

```
t e q o r s g u a
e y b p a w c o c
n u s o u n d h e
e s a v d b w g l
r o b c h s x u i
g n a e e t u q g
y r b k a f d b h
d e h p t n h o t
k g u b s t z f a
```

Which kind of energy provides power for many things we use? _____

© Houghton Mifflin Harcourt Publishing Company

Apply Concepts

Read each problem. Write the kind of energy you can use to solve it.

heat	light	sound

Discuss the Problem	Identify an Energy Solution
A soccer team wants to play a game at night.	_____
It is cold in the classroom.	_____
You want to know when someone is at the door.	_____

Take It Home!

Family Members: Ask your child to tell you about energy. Ask him or her to point out ways that energy is used around your home.

© Houghton Mifflin Harcourt Publishing Company

Essential Question

How Do Magnets Move Objects?

Engage Your Brain!

Find the answer to the question in the lesson.

What does a magnet do to iron and steel objects?

It _____ them.

Active Reading

Lesson Vocabulary

1. Preview the lesson.

2. Write the 4 vocabulary terms here.

_____   _____

_____   _____

© Houghton Mifflin Harcourt Publishing Company   (bg) ©Dave King/Dorling Kindersley/Getty Images

Inquiry Flipchart p. 20—Push and Pull/Which Magnet Will Win?

135

It's Magnetic

What is pulling the paper clips? It is a magnet. A **magnet** pulls iron or steel objects. It can push or pull other magnets, too. Magnets can have different strengths.

Active Reading

A detail is a fact about a main idea. Draw one line under a detail. Draw an arrow to the main idea it tells about.

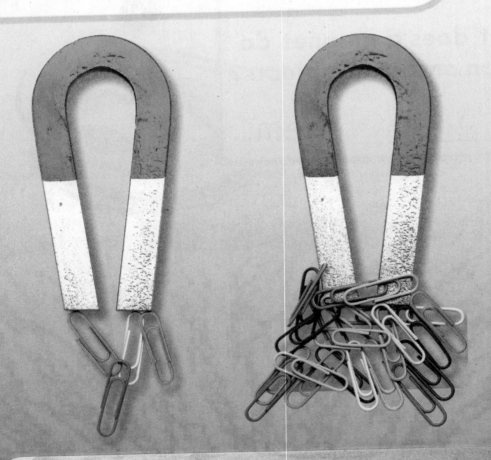

The magnet on the right is stronger. It pulls more than the other magnet.

© Houghton Mifflin Harcourt Publishing Company (bg) Alchemy/Alamy Images

Magnets have two poles. **Poles** are where the pull is the strongest. A magnet has an **N** pole and an **S** pole.

poles

▶Look at the magnet. Where is the pull the strongest?

_____

_____

© Houghton Mifflin Harcourt Publishing Company   (c) Alchemy/Alamy Images

Get Together

A magnet can attract things. **Attract** means to pull something. A magnet pulls things made of iron or steel. It can pull things without touching them.

not attracting

attracting

© Houghton Mifflin Harcourt Publishing Company

Opposite poles attract each other.
The N and S poles attract.

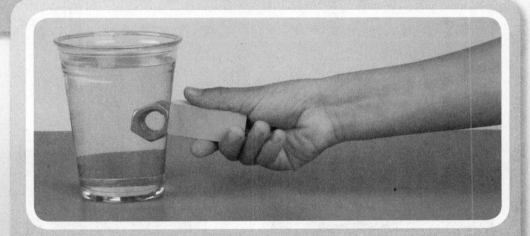

The magnet pulls the object through the cup and the water without touching it.

▶ Describe how a magnet can be used to pull an object.

_____

_____

© Houghton Mifflin Harcourt Publishing Company

Go Away!

A magnet does not always pull. Two magnets may repel. **Repel** means to push away. Like poles repel.

Active Reading

The main idea is the most important idea about something. Draw two lines under the main idea.

The two N poles and the two S poles repel each other.

© Houghton Mifflin Harcourt Publishing Company

▶ **Predict how this magnet could repel, or push, another magnet. Draw to show it.**

© Houghton Mifflin Harcourt Publishing Company

Sum It Up!

① Circle It!

Predict which object a magnet will attract. Circle it.

② Draw It!

In the first box, draw magnets attracting. In the second box, draw magnets repelling.

Attract	Repel

© Houghton Mifflin Harcourt Publishing Company (tl) PhotoDisc/Getty Images; (tc) ©Brand X Pictures/Getty Images

Brain Check

Lesson 2

Name _____

Word Play

Read each statement. Write your answer on the line below.

1 Describe what a magnet does when it attracts.

_____

2 Describe what a magnet does when it repels.

_____

3 Describe the poles of a magnet.

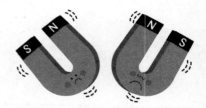

_____

© Houghton Mifflin Harcourt Publishing Company

Apply Concepts

Write the word that goes with each
set of clues.

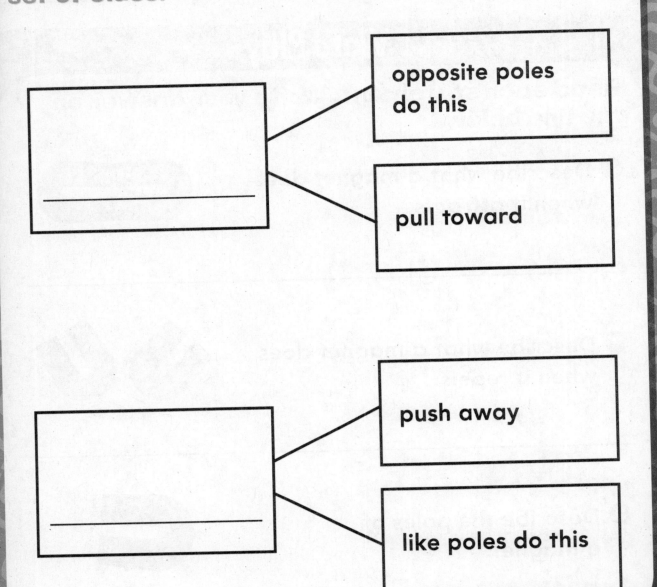

_____

opposite poles
do this

pull toward

_____

push away

like poles do this

 **Family Members:** Work with your child to identify household objects that a magnet will attract, as well as items it will not attract.

Take It Home!

© Houghton Mifflin Harcourt Publishing Company

Essential Question

How Do Objects Move?

🧠 Engage Your Brain!

Find the answer to the question in the lesson.

These Ferris wheel lights look blurry when they are in motion.

How does this Ferris wheel move?

_____

Active Reading

Lesson Vocabulary

❶ Preview the lesson.

❷ Write the 2 vocabulary terms here.

_____   _____

© Houghton Mifflin Harcourt Publishing Company   (bkg) ©Oleksiy Maksymenko/Alamy

Set Things in Motion

The log ride climbs up the hill slowly.

log ride

Look at all of the things in motion! **Motion** is movement. When something is in motion, it is moving. Up and down is one way that objects can move.

Planes fly fast. A turtle walks slowly. **Speed** is the measure of how fast something moves.

▶ Record the ways objects can move. Circle two things that move fast. Draw an X on two things that move slowly.

© Houghton Mifflin Harcourt Publishing Company

The log ride zooms down the hill fast.

Do the Math!
Make a Bar Graph

Pam went on three rides. This graph shows how long she waited for each ride.

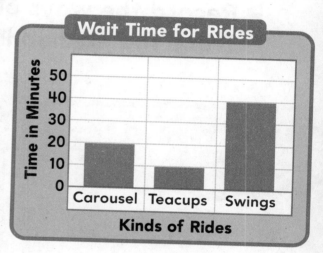

Wait Time for Rides

Time in Minutes

50
40
30
20
10
0

Carousel Teacups Swings

Kinds of Rides

Use the graph to answer the questions.

1. Which ride had the shortest wait?

_____

2. How does the graph tell you?

_____

© Houghton Mifflin Harcourt Publishing Company

It's Your Move!

Objects can move in other ways, too.
They can move in a straight line, zigzag,
back and forth, or round and round.

▶ **Record the ways objects can move.
Trace the dashed lines below.**

straight line

zigzag

© Houghton Mifflin Harcourt Publishing Company (bkgd) ©Martin Holtkamp/Getty Images

A detail is a fact about a main idea. Draw one line under a detail. Draw an arrow to the main idea it tells about.

back and forth

round and round

© Houghton Mifflin Harcourt Publishing Company

Sum It Up!

① Draw It!

Read the labels. Record how objects move. Draw an arrow to show the kind of motion.

back and forth	zigzag	round and round	straight line

② Circle It!

Look at each pair of objects. Circle the one that goes fast.

150

© Houghton Mifflin Harcourt Publishing Company

Brain Check

Name _____

Word Play

Work your way through the maze to match the word with its meaning.

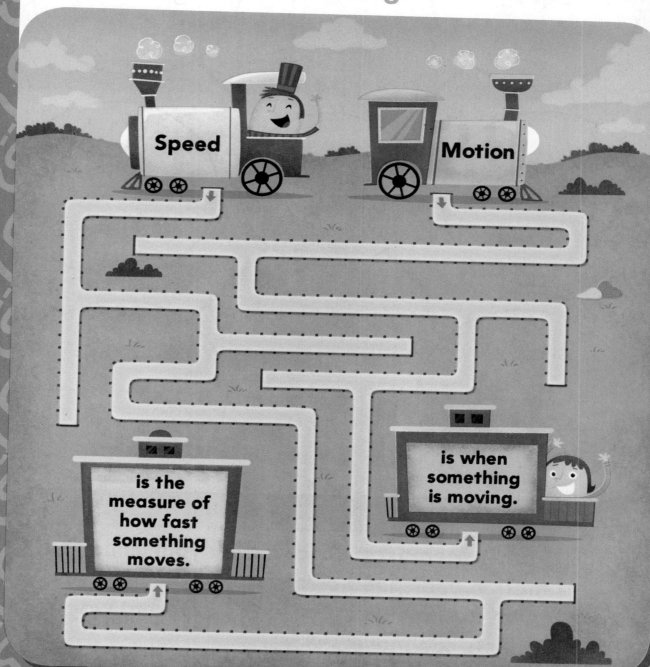

© Houghton Mifflin Harcourt Publishing Company

Apply Concepts

Complete the word web. Record how objects can move.

The Way Things Move

```
        zigzag                    _____


  _____        motion        _____


  _____                      _____
```

Take It Home!

Family Members: Discuss with your child the motion and speed of different objects. Ask them to show and record the different ways objects can move.

© Houghton Mifflin Harcourt Publishing Company

1

He is known for observing an apple falling from a tree.

2

He wrote his Three Laws of Motion.

4

Things to Know About

Isaac Newton

3

His laws help us understand why things move the way they do.

4

He was one of the greatest scientists in history.

© Houghton Mifflin Harcourt Publishing Company (bkgd) ©PhotoSlinger/Alamy; (bc) ©The Gallery Collection/Corbis; (br) ©Getty Images Royalty Free

eople in Science continued

Objects in Motion

Think about what you know about Isaac Newton. Then write the answer to each question.

What did Isaac Newton write after seeing an apple fall from a tree?

_____

_____

What is Isaac Newton remembered as?

_____

_____

What do the Three Laws of Motion tell us?

_____

_____

© Houghton Mifflin Harcourt Publishing Company

Inquiry Flipchart p. 22

TEKS **1.2A** ask questions about organisms, objects, and events observed the natural world **1.2B** plan and conduc simple descriptive investigations such as ways objects move **1.2D** record and organize data using pictures, numbers, an words **1.6D** demonstrate and record the ways that objects can move such as in a straight line, zig zag, up and down, back and forth, round and round, and fast and slow

Name _____

Essential Question

How Can We Move a Ball?

Set a Purpose

Tell what you will do in this investigation.

_____

Think About the Procedure

❶ What kinds of motion will you show?

_____

_____

❷ How will you show the motion?

_____

_____

© Houghton Mifflin Harcourt Publishing Company

Record Your Data

Draw to record what you did.

Motion	Drawing
Straight line	
Zigzag	
Back and forth	
Round and round	
Up and down	

Draw Conclusions

How can a ball move? How do you know?

_____

_____

Ask More Questions

What questions can you ask about how objects move?

_____

_____

© Houghton Mifflin Harcourt Publishing Company

Essential Question

How Can We Change the Way Objects Move?

Engage Your Brain!

Find the answer to the question in the lesson.

How is pushing a swing like pulling a wagon?

A push and a pull are both

_____.

Active Reading

Lesson Vocabulary

1 Preview the lesson.

2 Write the 3 vocabulary terms here.

_____   _____

_____

© Houghton Mifflin Harcourt Publishing Company (bkgd) ©Fay Bottarel/Getty Images

In Full Force

What makes the wagon move? The girl gives it a push. A **push** moves an object away from you. The boy gives the wagon a pull. A **pull** moves an object closer to you.

Pushes and pulls are forces. A **force** makes an object move or stop moving. When the girl and boy push and pull the wagon, it starts to move.

▶ **Draw yourself pushing something.**

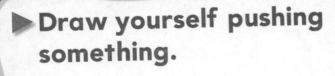

© Houghton Mifflin Harcourt Publishing Company

▶ Draw yourself
pulling something.

Active Reading

Find the sentence that tells the meaning
of **force**. Draw a line under the sentence.

© Houghton Mifflin Harcourt Publishing Company

Using Force

Look at the pictures. How does a force move a ball? A force can change the way an object moves. It can change a ball's speed or location.

Changing Speed

Force can change an object's speed. It can make something start moving or stop moving. It can make something go faster or more slowly.

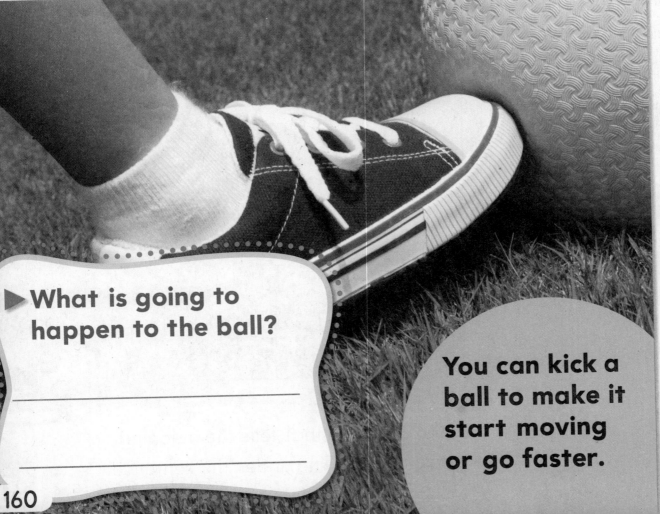

▶ **What is going to happen to the ball?**

_____

_____

You can kick a ball to make it start moving or go faster.

© Houghton Mifflin Harcourt Publishing Company

You can catch
a ball to stop it.

▶ Describe how the motion of the cars change.

1   2   3

1 _____

2 _____

3 _____

© Houghton Mifflin Harcourt Publishing Company

Changing Location

The toys are in different places. Some are nearer, or closer, to the yellow truck. Others are farther from it.

Nearer, closer, and **farther** are location words. Location tells where something is. A force can move something to a new location.

Active Reading

A detail is a fact about a main idea. Draw one line under a detail. Draw an arrow to the main idea it tells about.

The green truck is closer to the yellow truck.

A force moved it farther from the yellow truck.

© Houghton Mifflin Harcourt Publishing Company

What's Your Location?

Think about pushing a friend on a swing. Your friend moves farther from you and then comes nearer, or closer. Forces can move things closer to and farther from you.

▶ **Describe how this swing changes location as it moves.**

_____

_____

_____

© Houghton Mifflin Harcourt Publishing Company   (bkgd) ©Reed Kaestner/Corbis

What Makes That Coaster Move?

Roller coasters are fun! They go up and down, fast and slow, round and round. People on the ride might yell as they change speed and location. What makes the coaster move?

A motor pulls a chain. The chain pulls the car up the first hill.

© Houghton Mifflin Harcourt Publishing Company (bkgd) ©John Zsitner/Getty Images; (br) © Wm Baker/ GhostWorx Images / Alamy

Gravity is the force that pulls the car down. Gravity pulls all things toward Earth.

► **What pulls the car down the hill?**

_____

© Houghton Mifflin Harcourt Publishing Company

Sum It Up!

① Solve It!

Write the word that solves the riddle.

I move a box
when it is full.
I can be a push
or a pull.

What am I?

_____

② Circle It!

Forces can change objects. Circle the words that tell the kinds of changes.

speed   color

size   location

shape

③ Label It!

Describe the ball's change in location. Write <u>nearer to</u> or <u>farther from</u> below each picture.

_____   _____

© Houghton Mifflin Harcourt Publishing Company

Name _____

Word Play

Complete the letter by using these words.

speed force	push closer	pull farther

Dear Jen,

Yesterday my brother and I played trains. The front car can _____ other cars. I gave my train a _____. It moved _____ from me. It moved _____ to my brother. My brother sent the train down a hill. The _____ made it go so fast! It picked up _____ as it went down. It was fun to make the trains move!

Your friend,

Amy

© Houghton Mifflin Harcourt Publishing Company

Apply Concepts

Complete the chart. Write a word on each blank line.

nearer to   farther from   location

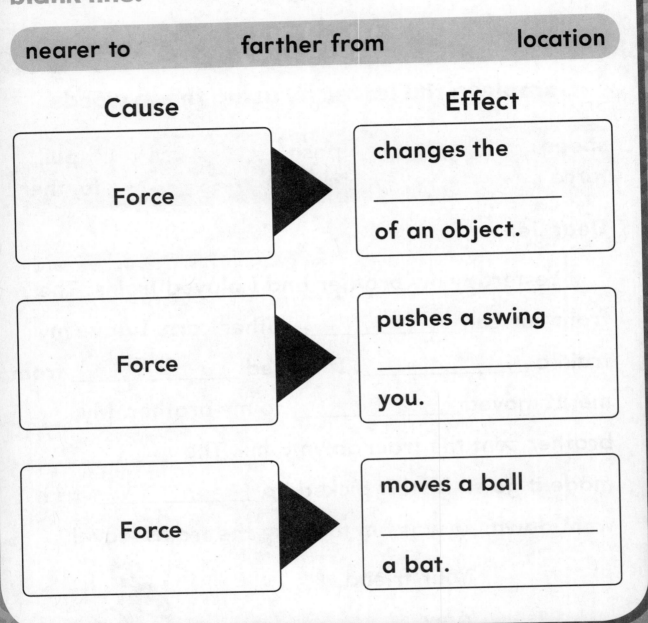

Cause   **Effect**

Cause	Effect
Force	changes the _____ of an object.
Force	pushes a swing _____ you.
Force	moves a ball _____ a bat.

Take It Home!

Family Members: Ask your child to tell you about forces and motion. Have your child point out examples of pushes and pulls and explain how those forces change motion.

© Houghton Mifflin Harcourt Publishing Company

TEKS 1.3A identify and explain a problem such as finding a home for a classroom pet and propose a solution in his/her own words

Fly to the Sky

The First Flight

Wilbur and Orville Wright were brothers and inventors. They had a problem. The brothers wanted to fly an airplane. Together they came up with a solution. First, they made designs of their plane. Next, they built it. Then, they tested it. After a few tries, their plane flew.

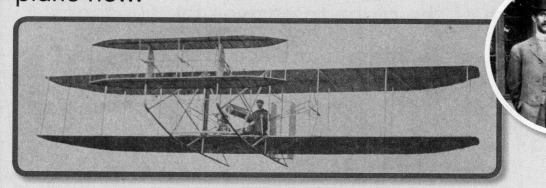

This is one of the Wright Brothers' planes.

Today's planes look different and have more parts.

© Houghton Mifflin Harcourt Publishing Company (cl) ©Mary Evans Picture Library/Photo Researchers, Inc.; (inset) ©Pictorial Press Ltd/Alamy; (br) ©Colin Underhill/Alamy

Plane Parts

Each part of a plane has a job to do. The wings help lift it. The tail keeps it flying straight. The propeller moves the plane forward.

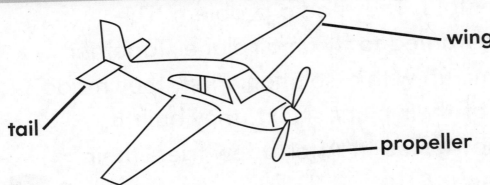

tail

wing

propeller

Use the picture of the plane to answer the questions.

1 Which part keeps the plane flying straight? Circle it.

2 What would happen if the wings on the plane were missing? Explain.

_____

_____

Build On It!

Build your own paper airplanes. Complete **Build It: Paper Airplanes** on the Inquiry Flipchart.

© Houghton Mifflin Harcourt Publishing Company (f) ©Rich Reid/National Geographic/Getty Images

Vocabulary Review

Use the terms in the box to complete the sentences.

> heat
> magnet
> motion

1. If something is moving, it is in

   _____.

TEKS 1.6A

2. _____ is a kind of energy people use to keep warm.

TEKS 1.6B

3. A _____ can pull objects made of iron or steel.

Science Concepts

Fill in the letter of the choice that best answers the question.

TEKS 1.6D

4. A ball is hanging from a string. You pull the ball back and let it go. What kind of motion does the ball make?

   Ⓐ back and forth

   Ⓑ round and round

   Ⓒ straight line

TEKS 1.6A

5. Which sentence identifies a way that sound energy is important?

   Ⓐ It lets people cook food.

   Ⓑ It can warn people of danger.

   Ⓒ It gives people light to see at night.

© Houghton Mifflin Harcourt Publishing Company

Which kinds of energy is the fire giving off? Identify them.

Ⓐ heat and sound
Ⓑ light and heat
Ⓒ light and sound

7. Which of these objects needs electricity to work?
Ⓐ a baseball bat
Ⓑ a lamp
Ⓒ a marker

8. What can a force do?
Ⓐ stop an object
Ⓑ move an object
Ⓒ move or stop an object

9. Which of these objects will a magnet attract? Predict it.

Ⓐ

Ⓑ

Ⓒ

© Houghton Mifflin Harcourt Publishing Company

10. Which do you move round and round on?

Ⓐ a merry-go-round

Ⓑ a slide

Ⓒ a swing

11. You can describe how the location of an object changes. How does the ball's location change when the boy throws it?

Ⓐ The ball moves closer to the boy.

Ⓑ The ball moves farther from the boy.

Ⓒ The ball stays in the same place.

12. What question does the picture answer?

Ⓐ How can a ball move?

Ⓑ Who wins the game?

Ⓒ Is the ball filled with air?

© Houghton Mifflin Harcourt Publishing Company

Inquiry and the Big Idea

Write the answers to these questions.

TEKS 1.4A, 1.6B

13. Compare the magnets. Describe what they are doing. How do you know?

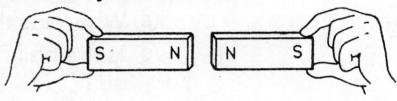

_____

_____

TEKS 1.6C, 1.6D

14. Look at the picture.

a. What kind of force is being put on the ball? Describe how the location of the ball will change.

_____

_____

b. Name two things that the force can change about the ball.

_____

© Houghton Mifflin Harcourt Publishing Company

UNIT 5
Earth's Resources

Big Idea
There are many kinds of resources on Earth.

TEKS 1.1C, 1.2A, 1.2B, 1.2D, 1.3A, 1.3C, 1.7A, 1.7B, 1.7C

sandy beach

© Houghton Mifflin Harcourt Publishing Company (bg) ©iStock/Getty Images; (border) ©NDisc/Age Fotostock

I Wonder Why
Trash on the beach needs to be cleaned up. Why?
Turn the page to find out.

Here's Why Trash can be harmful to land, water, and living things at the beach.

In this unit, you will explore this Big Idea, the Essential Questions, and the Investigations on the Inquiry Flipchart.

Levels of Inquiry Key ■ DIRECTED ■ GUIDED ■ INDEPENDENT

Track Your Progress

Big Idea There are many kinds of resources on Earth.

Essential Questions

Lesson 1 What Can We Find on Earth? 177
Inquiry Flipchart p. 25—Just Add Water/Resources All Around

🔁 **People in Science:** Dr. George Washington Carver 187

Lesson 2 What Is Soil? 189
Inquiry Flipchart p. 26—Cleaning Crew/How Much Water?

Inquiry Lesson 3 What Do We Find in Soil? 199
Inquiry Flipchart p. 27—What Do We Find in Soil?

Inquiry Lesson 4 How Do Soils Differ? 201
Inquiry Flipchart p. 28—How Do Soils Differ?

Lesson 5 Where Can We Find Water? 203
Inquiry Flipchart p. 29—Pass the Salt?/Water Watch

S.T.E.M. Engineering and Technology: Technology and the Environment 215
Inquiry Flipchart p. 30—Design It: Water Filter

Lesson 6 How Can We Save Resources? 217
Inquiry Flipchart p. 31—Trash on the Grass/Ready, Set, Recycle!

Unit 5 Review 229

Now I Get the Big Idea!

Science Notebook

Before you begin each lesson, be sure to write your thoughts about the Essential Question.

© Houghton Mifflin Harcourt Publishing Company (bg) ©Vstock/Getty Images (border) ©NDisc/Age Fotostock

TEKS **1.1C** identify and learn how to use natural resources and materials, including conservation and reuse or recycling of paper, plastic, and metals **1.7C** gather evidence of how rocks, soil, and water help to make useful products

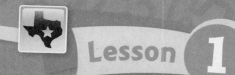

Essential Question

What Can We Find on Earth?

Engage Your Brain!

Find the answer in the lesson.

The Great Sphinx was built long ago.

It was built from

_____.

Active Reading

Lesson Vocabulary

1 Preview the lesson.

2 Write the 4 vocabulary terms here.

_____   _____

_____   _____

© Houghton Mifflin Harcourt Publishing Company   (bkgd) Clinspires/ack/Corbis

Inquiry Flipchart p. 25 — Just Add Water/Resources All Around

All Natural

What do you use from Earth? You use natural resources. A **natural resource** is anything from nature that people can use.

Air

Air is a natural resource. We breathe air. Wind is moving air. This hang glider uses wind to move. A wind farm changes wind into useful energy. Energy gives light and heat to our homes.

Active Reading

Draw two lines under the main idea.

© Houghton Mifflin Harcourt Publishing Company (bkgd) ©Chris Cheadle/Alamy; (inset) ©Martin Jenkinson/Alamy

Water

We use water every day. We drink it and bathe with it. Water also helps to make useful products, such as shampoo. A **product** is something made by people or machines for people to use.

There is water in this iced tea.

There is water in this lotion.

We use water to care for plants.

▶ Identify a product made with water. Tell why it is useful.

_____

_____

_____

© Houghton Mifflin Harcourt Publishing Company   (tl) ©Plush Studios/Getty Images; (tr) ©Yellow Dog Productions/Photographer's Choice/Getty Images; (inset) ©Nick Koudis/Photodisc/Getty Images

Plants and Animals

Plants and animals are natural resources, too. We use them for food. We also use them to make clothes and other things we need.

▶ **Look at the pictures. Circle the useful product that comes from each plant or animal.**

We make socks from cotton.

We make wood toys from trees.

We make food from tomatoes.

180

© Houghton Mifflin Harcourt Publishing Company

We make a sweater from a sheep's wool.

We make cheese from a cow's milk.

We get eggs from a hen.

© Houghton Mifflin Harcourt Publishing Company

Rocks

Rocks are a natural resource. A **rock** is a hard, nonliving object from the ground. We use rocks to build things. Rocks can also be used to make useful products like jewelry or salt.

Active Reading

Find the sentence that tells the meaning of **rock.** Draw a line under the sentence.

house made from rocks

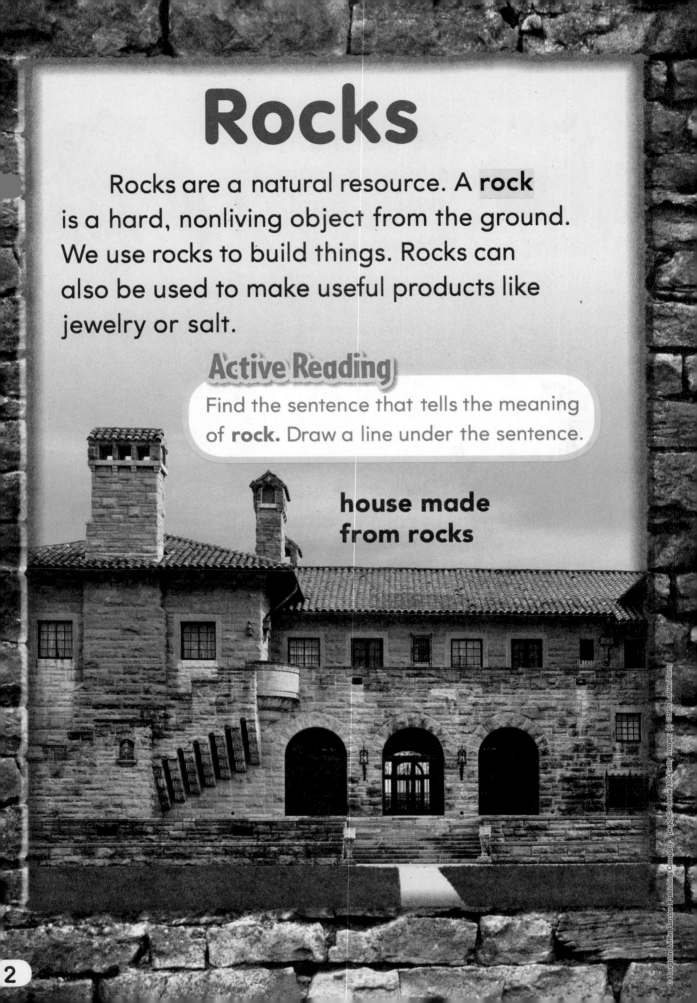

© Houghton Mifflin Harcourt Publishing Company (bkgd) Andrew Holt/Getty Images; (b) Geri LaRue/Alamy

Soil

Soil is a natural resource, too. **Soil** is made up of small pieces of rock and once-living things. It is the top layer of Earth. We use soil to grow plants. We can also use it to make useful products. Soil can be made into bricks for building.

▶Identify two natural resources on these pages.

_____

© Houghton Mifflin Harcourt Publishing Company (t) ©David Salman/Corbis

Sum It Up!

① Write It!

Solve the riddle.

How are a , 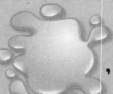, and a  alike?

They are all _____.

② Circle It!

Circle the product made from each resource.

Plant	Rock	Water	Soil

© Houghton Mifflin Harcourt Publishing Company

Name _____

Word Play

Write the word that completes each sentence.

soil	rock	natural resource

1 A $\underset{1}{\bigcirc}$ _ _ _ is a nonliving object from the ground.

2 You can use _ $\underset{2}{\bigcirc}$ _ _ to grow plants.

3 A _ _ $\underset{5}{\bigcirc}\underset{3}{\bigcirc}$ _ _ _ _ _ _ $\underset{4}{\bigcirc}$ _

is something from nature that you can use.

Use the circled letters to answer the clue.

I am something people or machines
make for people to use.

I am a p __ __ d __ __ __.
     1   2   3   4   5

© Houghton Mifflin Harcourt Publishing Company

Apply Concepts

Identify natural resources. Fill in the organizer.

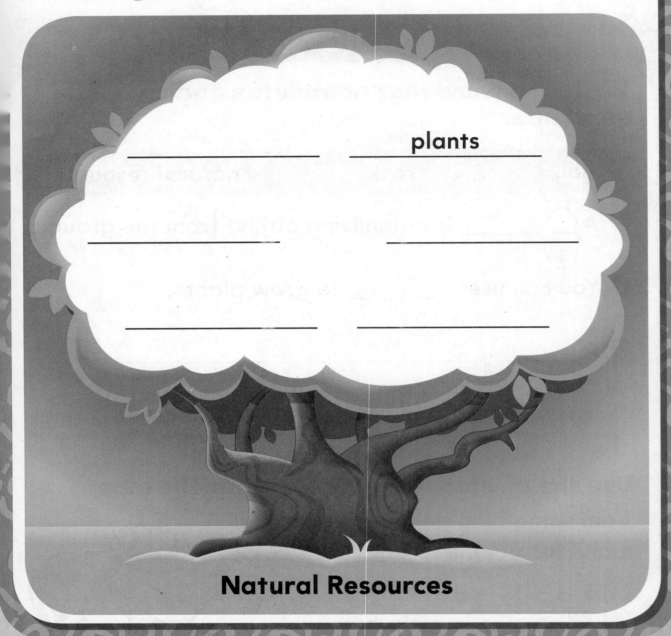

plants

_____   _____

_____   _____

_____   _____

Natural Resources

Take It Home!

Family Members: Work with your child to identify things in your home that are products made from natural resources.

© Houghton Mifflin Harcourt Publishing Company

Learn About...
Dr. George Washington Carver

Dr. George Washington Carver was a scientist. He worked with farmers. Dr. Carver showed them how to plant peanuts to keep their soil good for growing crops.

Fun Fact

Dr. Carver invented peanut shampoo!

© Houghton Mifflin Harcourt Publishing Company   (bkgd) ©Creativ Studio Heinemann/Westend61/Corbis; (bl) ©Stock Montage/Getty Images

This Leads to That

Dr. George Washington Carver studied farming.

He taught farmers how to make their soil rich.

Today, farmers around the world use his ideas.

► **Describe what Dr. Carver did to help farmers.**

_____

_____

_____

© Houghton Mifflin Harcourt Publishing Company (cl) ©Corbis; (c) ©Corbis; (tr) ©Bettmann/Corbis; (br) ©C Squared Studios/Getty Images; ©C Squared Studios/Getty Images/PhotoDisc

Essential Question

What Is Soil?

Find the answer to the question in the lesson.

How can people use soil?

to _____

Active Reading

Lesson Vocabulary

❶ Preview the lesson.

❷ Write the 5 vocabulary terms here.

_____ _____

_____ _____

_____

© Houghton Mifflin Harcourt Publishing Company ©Pierre Rosberg/Getty Images

Super Soil

Soil is made up of small pieces of rock and once-living things. We use soil to grow plants.

Active Reading

Find the sentence that tells the meaning of **soil**. Draw a line under the sentence.

Soil forms a layer on parts of Earth's surface.

© Houghton Mifflin Harcourt Publishing Company   ©Mike Grandmaison/Corbis

Soil forms when wind and water break down rock. The bits of rock form the base of soil.

At the same time, dead plants and animals fall to the ground. These once-living things break down into bits. The bits become part of soil, too.

Soil is a mix of many tiny pieces.

▶ **Look at the picture. Describe the color and texture of the soil.**

_____

_____

© Houghton Mifflin Harcourt Publishing Company © Mike Grandmaison/Corbis

The Scoop on Soil

Sand, silt, clay, and once-living things make up soil. Different amounts of these parts make soils different.

Active Reading

Find the sentence that tells what **sand** is made of. Draw a line under the sentence.

Farm soil has many once-living things.

© Houghton Mifflin Harcourt Publishing Company (bkgd) ©Digital Vision/Getty Images

Soil is a mix of these four parts.

Sand is made of large bits of rock. It does not hold water well.

Silt is made of medium bits of rock. It holds water fairly well.

Clay is made of small bits of rock. Clay holds water so well that clay sticks together.

Once-living things are bits of dead plants and animals. They make soil rich, or good for plants.

▶ **Circle the part of soil that makes soil good for growing plants.**

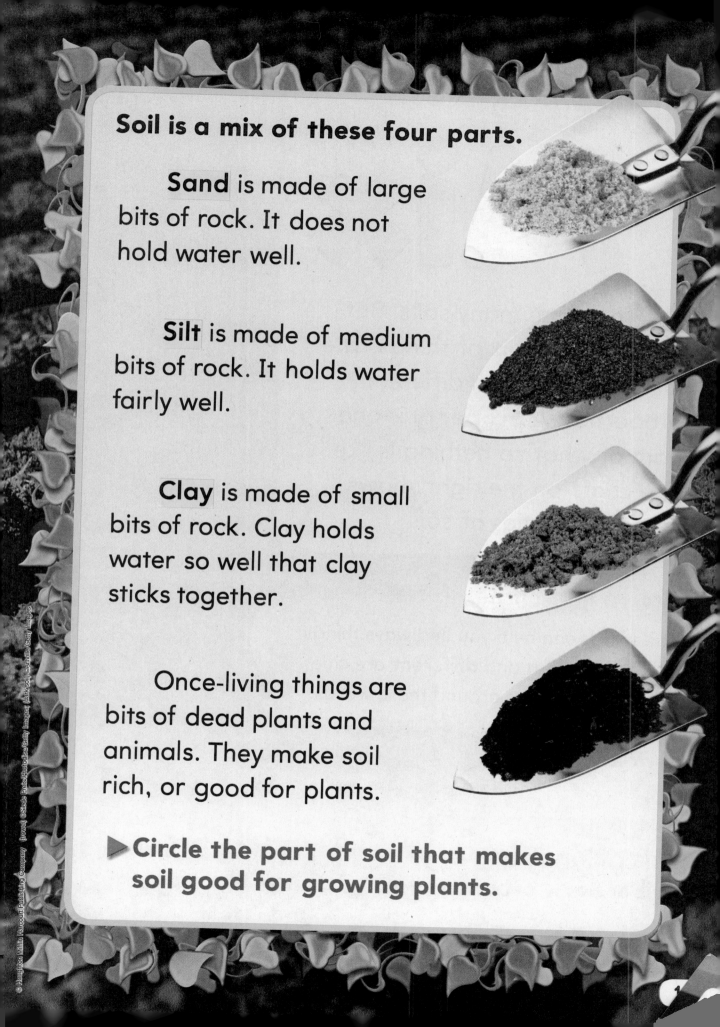

© Houghton Mifflin Harcourt Publishing Company (Iowa) ©Stsde Preis/Photodics/Getty Images (darksoil) ©Arville/Getty Images

In the Mix

There are many soils. But each soil is a mix of things. The mix gives each soil different properties. A **property** is one part of what something is like. The chart on the right shows some properties of soil.

Active Reading

Clue words can help you find ways things are different. **But** and **different** are clue words. Draw boxes around these words.

This rich garden soil is dark brown.

© Houghton Mifflin Harcourt Publishing Company

► **Compare and describe the parts of soil.**
Write labels to complete the chart.

Color The rock in soil helps give soil its color.
Soil can be orange, gray, tan, and yellow, too.

red   _____   black

Size of Rock Bits The rock bits may be different
sizes. Clay has small bits. Sand has large ones.

small   medium   _____

Texture The size and shape of the rock bits
make soils feel different.

_____   gritty   lumpy

Amount of Once-Living Things Once-living
things make soil rich. Rich soil is good for plants.

few   _____   many

© Houghton Mifflin Harcourt Publishing Company

Sum It Up!

① Write It!

List the four parts that make up soil.

_____

_____

_____

_____

② Order It!

Write 1, 2, 3 to order how a plant becomes part of soil.

___ The plant begins to break into pieces.

___ A plant dies and falls to the ground.

___ The pieces get smaller and become part of soil.

③ Draw It!

Draw soil that has these properties.

tan   large rock bits   gritty   few once-living things

Dig it!

© Houghton Mifflin Harcourt Publishing Company

Brain Check

Name _____

Word Play

Observe and compare the parts of soil.
Match each part of soil to its description.
Then add a detail about the size of rock bits.

sand

It holds water so well that it sticks together.

_____

_____

silt

It does not hold water well.

_____

_____

clay

It holds water fairly well.

_____

_____

© Houghton Mifflin Harcourt Publishing Company

Apply Concepts

Fill in the chart. Describe how soil forms.

How Soil Forms

```
┌─────────────────────────────────────┐
│                                      │
│  ──────────────────────────────────  │
│                                      │
│  ──────────────────────────────────  │
│                                      │
└─────────────────────────────────────┘
                  │
                  ▼
┌─────────────────────────────────────┐
│                                      │
│  ──────────────────────────────────  │
│                                      │
│  ──────────────────────────────────  │
│                                      │
└─────────────────────────────────────┘
                  │
                  ▼
┌─────────────────────────────────────┐
│  All the bits mix together to make   │
│  soil.                               │
└─────────────────────────────────────┘
```

Take It Home!

Family Members: Walk with your child near your home to observe soil. Have your child describe and compare the parts of soil.

© Houghton Mifflin Harcourt Publishing Company

TEKS **1.2A** ask questions about organisms, objects, and events observe the natural world **1.2B** plan and condu simple descriptive investigations such as ways objects move **1.2D** record and organize data using pictures, numbers, words **1.7A** observe, compare, describe and sort components of soil by size, text and color

Name _____

Essential Question
What Do We Find in Soil?

Set a Purpose
Tell what you want to find out.

_____

_____

Think About the Procedure
❶ What tools do you have?

_____

❷ Tell about one way you will use a tool to separate the soil into parts.

_____

_____

© Houghton Mifflin Harcourt Publishing Company

Record Your Data

Draw and label the parts in your soil sample.

Draw Conclusions

What parts make up your soil?

_____

_____

Ask More Questions

What other questions can you ask about soil?

_____

_____

© Houghton Mifflin Harcourt Publishing Company

Inquiry Flipchart p. 28

TEKS **1.2A** ask questions about organisms, objects, and events observe the natural world **1.2B** plan and condu simple descriptive investigations such as ways objects move **1.2D** record and organize data using pictures, numbers, a words **1.7A** observe, compare, describe and sort components of soil by size, text and color

Name _____

Essential Question

How Do Soils Differ?

Set a Purpose

Tell what you want to find out.

_____

_____

Think About the Procedure

❶ How many soil samples will you compare?

_____

❷ Name some properties of soil that you will observe.

_____

_____

_____

© Houghton Mifflin Harcourt Publishing Company

Record Your Data

Describe and sort the parts of soil. Draw and write to record what you observe.

Property	Soil Sample 1	Soil Sample 2
Color		
Texture		
Size of Bits		

Draw Conclusions

Compare. How are the soils the same and different?

_____

_____

_____

Ask More Questions

What other questions could you ask about the different parts of soil?

_____

© Houghton Mifflin Harcourt Publishing Company

Essential Question

Where Can We Find Water?

🧠 Engage Your Brain!

Find the answer to the question in the lesson.

How much of Earth is covered with water?

_____

Active Reading

Lesson Vocabulary

① Preview the lesson.

② Write the 4 vocabulary terms here.

_____   _____

_____   _____

© Houghton Mifflin Harcourt Publishing Company (bkgd) ©NASA/K. Horgan/Stone/Getty Images

So Fresh

Most plants and animals need fresh water. People need fresh water, too. Fresh water is not salty. You can find sources of fresh water in many places.

streams

A **stream** is a small body of flowing water.

rivers

Some streams flow into rivers. A **river** is a large body of flowing water.

© Houghton Mifflin Harcourt Publishing Company (l) ©Frank Krahmer/Corbis (r) ©Tori Richardson/Robert Harding World Imagery/Corbis

► **Look at the pictures. Identify the three bodies of water. Circle their names. Describe each one by drawing a line under a sentence that tells about it.**

lakes

A **lake** is a body of water with land all around it. Water in a lake does not flow.

© Houghton Mifflin Harcourt Publishing Company ©Theo Allofs/Corbis

So Salty

You can find water in oceans too. An **ocean** is a large body of salty water. Most of Earth's water is in oceans.

Active Reading

A detail is a fact about a main idea. Draw one line under a detail. Draw an arrow to the main idea it tells about.

▶ **Identify the body of water you see on the page. Circle the name of it. Describe the body of water by writing a sentence about it.**

_____

© Houghton Mifflin Harcourt Publishing Company ©David Puu/Corbis

surfer in ocean

Do the Math!
Model Fractions

About $\frac{3}{4}$, or three fourths, of Earth is covered with water. The rest is covered with land.

This circle models Earth's water and land. It has 4 parts. Color the parts to show how much water is on Earth.

Now look at the circle. How much of Earth is covered with land?

Answer: _____

© Houghton Mifflin Harcourt Publishing Company

Wonderful Water

All living things need water. Plants, animals, and people need it to stay healthy.

Active Reading

The main idea is the most important idea about something. Draw two lines under the main idea.

People drink water.

Animals drink water.

© Houghton Mifflin Harcourt Publishing Company (bkg) ©Paul A. Souders/Corbis; (bl) ©PatitucciPhoto/Getty Images; (br) ©Frans Lanting/Corbis

Save Earth's water!

We must protect water and keep it clean.

Follow these tips to help.

1 Use less water for baths and showers.

2 Fix leaky pipes or faucets.

3 Put trash in trash cans! Do not put trash in water.

Water flows through this dam.

Plants need water too.

▶ **Add your own tip for protecting Earth's water.**

_____

_____

_____

© Houghton Mifflin Harcourt Publishing Company   (t) ©Steve Satushek/Stone/Getty Images

Jump into Safety!

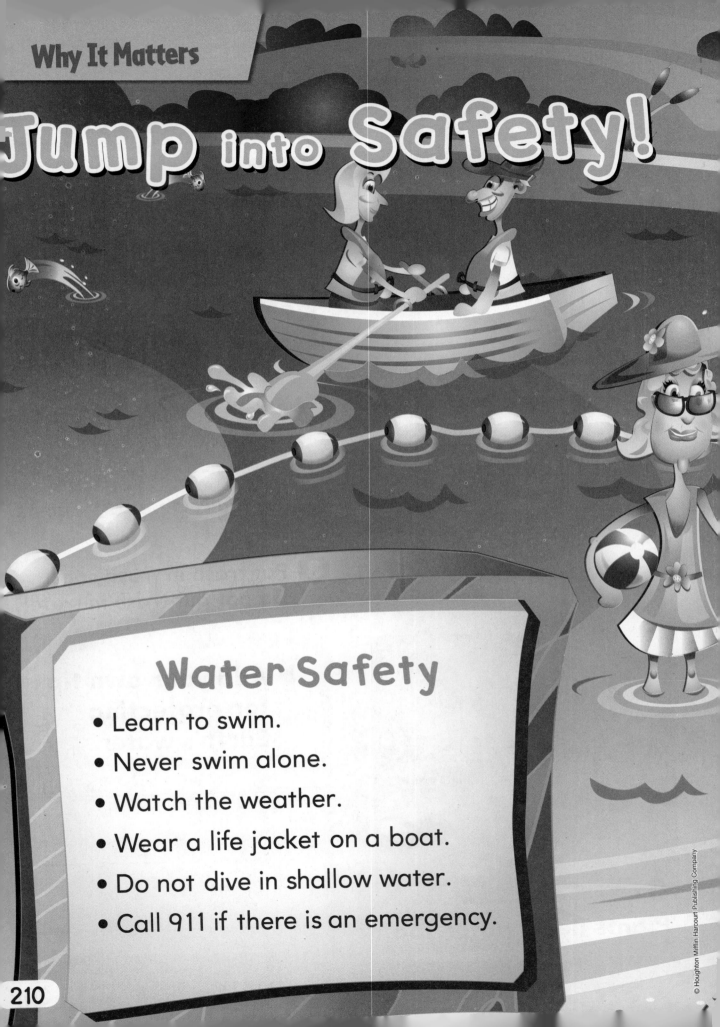

Water Safety

- Learn to swim.
- Never swim alone.
- Watch the weather.
- Wear a life jacket on a boat.
- Do not dive in shallow water.
- Call 911 if there is an emergency.

© Houghton Mifflin Harcourt Publishing Company

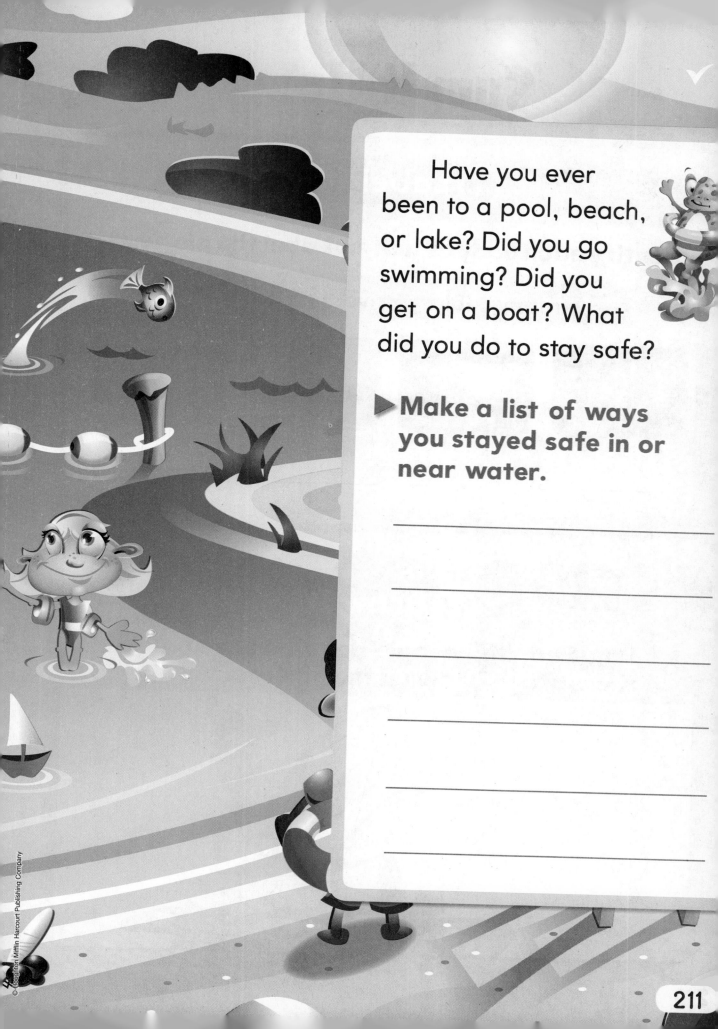

Have you ever been to a pool, beach, or lake? Did you go swimming? Did you get on a boat? What did you do to stay safe?

▶ **Make a list of ways you stayed safe in or near water.**

_____

_____

_____

_____

_____

© Houghton Mifflin Harcourt Publishing Company

Sum It Up!

① Label It!

Identify each body of water. Label the pictures.

stream   lake   river   ocean

_____   _____   _____   _____

② Draw It!

What can the people do to be safe on the water? Draw on the picture.

© Houghton Mifflin Harcourt Publishing Company

Word Play

Fill in the blanks. Use these words to describe the different bodies of water.

| ocean | lake | stream | river | fresh water |

Most lakes have __ __ __ __ __ __ ◯ __ __ __ __ .

An __ __ __ ◯ __ has salty water.

A __ ◯ __ __ __ __ __ is a small body of water.

A __ __ __ ◯ has water that does not flow.

Streams can flow together to make a ◯ __ __ __ __ .

Then use the circled letters to fill in the blanks below.

We use __ __ __ __ __ in many ways!

© Houghton Mifflin Harcourt Publishing Company

Apply Concepts

Write your answer to each question.

1 Why do we need water?

_____

_____

_____

2 How can we stay safe around water?

• _____

• _____

• _____

• _____

Take It Home!

Family Members: Help your child to identify and describe different bodies of water. Then work with your child to identify ways to save water at home.

© Houghton Mifflin Harcourt Publishing Company

TEKS 1.3A identify and explain a problem such as finding a home for a classroom pet and propose a solution in his/her own words

Technology and the Environment

Dams

A dam is a wall built across a river. It slows the flow of the river. A dam can be helpful. It is built to help solve problems. It can provide water for drinking and for crops. It can also control floods.

A dam can also harm the environment. Fish, like salmon, can not move across some dams. Some animals lose their homes.

© Houghton Mifflin Harcourt Publishing Company (bl) ©Bettmann/Corbis; (inset) ©Kevin Fleming/Corbis

S.T.E.M.
continued

Helpful and Harmful

How are dams helpful? How are dams harmful? Use your ideas to complete the chart.

Effects of Dams	
Helpful	Harmful

Build On It!

Learn more about water and technology. Complete **Design It: Water Filter** on the Inquiry Flipchart.

© Houghton Mifflin Harcourt Publishing Company (t) ©U.S. Bureau of Reclamation/Photo Researchers, Inc.

Lesson **6**

Essential Question

How Can We Save Resources?

Engage Your Brain!

Find the answer to the question in the lesson.

This art uses old things to make something new. How does this help Earth?

It makes less

_____.

Active Reading

Lesson Vocabulary

1 Preview the lesson.

2 Write the 5 vocabulary terms here.

_____   _____

_____   _____

_____

Inquiry Flipchart p. 31—Trash on the Grass/Ready, Set, Recycle!

217

© Houghton Mifflin Harcourt Publishing Company · (t) ©Andrea Jones/Alamy

What a Waste!

Pollution is waste that harms land, water, and air. It can make people and animals sick. Plants can be harmed, too. Pollution makes water unsafe to drink. It also makes the air dirty. Dirty air is unsafe to breathe. We all need clean resources.

Active Reading

Find the sentence that tells the meaning of **pollution**. Draw a line under the sentence.

© Houghton Mifflin Harcourt Publishing Company

Draw a circle on the air pollution.
Draw an X on the land pollution.
Draw a box on the water pollution.

© Houghton Mifflin Harcourt Publishing Company

Pollution Solutions

People can keep land, water, and air clean. They can put trash in trash cans. People can keep waste away from water. They can drive less to keep the air clean.

Conservation is a way to protect natural resources and materials. When you conserve something, you use less of it.

▶ **Look at the pictures in each row. Write <u>land</u>, <u>water</u>, or <u>air</u> to complete each sentence.**

© Houghton Mifflin Harcourt Publishing Company

How to Help

People ride bikes.
This keeps the
_____ clean.

People keep waste
out of the river.
This keeps the
_____ clean.

People put trash in
cans. This keeps the
_____ clean.

© Houghton Mifflin Harcourt Publishing Company

Care for Earth!

You can learn how to reduce, reuse, and recycle natural resources and materials. This makes less trash.

To **reduce** is to use less of something. You use less water when you turn the faucet off. To **reuse** is to use something again. You can reuse a can to make a pencil holder. To **recycle** is to use old things to make new things. You can recycle the plastic in bottles to make something new.

© Houghton Mifflin Harcourt Publishing Company

Active Reading

An effect tells what happens. Draw two lines under an effect of **reducing**, **reusing**, and **recycling**.

© Houghton Mifflin Harcourt Publishing Company

Good As New

Have you ever worn a shirt made from plastic bottles? Have you ever reused a plastic milk jug as a bird feeder? We can recycle and reuse many old things. Metal from cans may be recycled to make a new baseball bat. A metal can may also be reused as a planter. Paper can be reused and recycled, too.

▶ **Match each object on the left to what it became on the right.**

1 milk jug

2 newspaper

3 cans

© Houghton Mifflin Harcourt Publishing Company (c) ©Ryan McVay/Photodisc/Getty Images

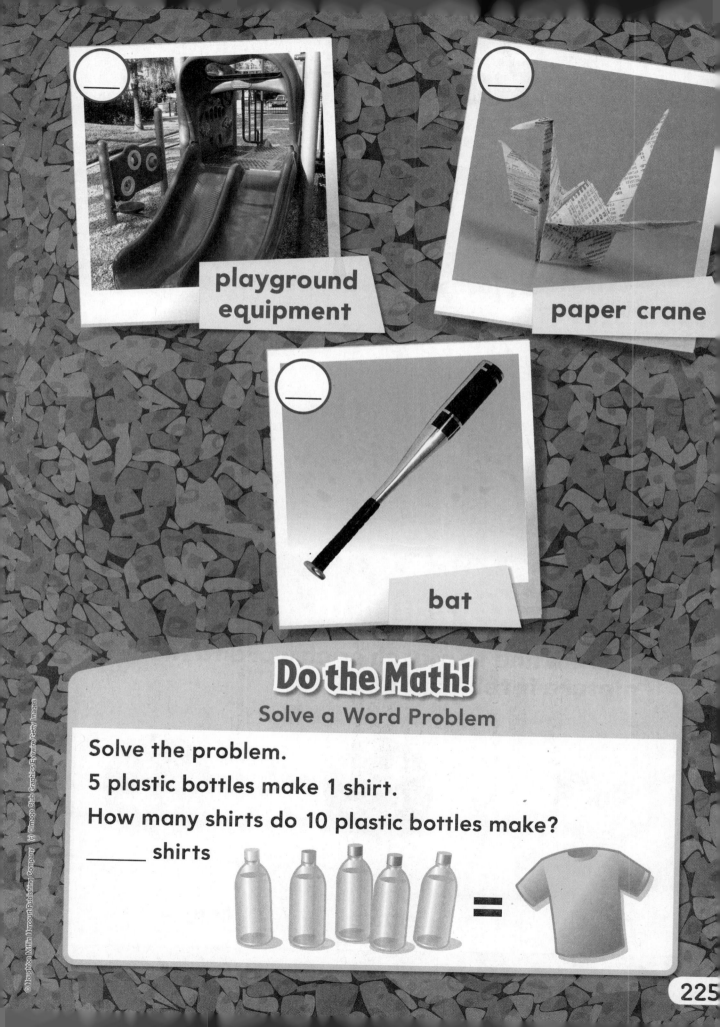

playground
equipment

paper crane

bat

Do the Math!
Solve a Word Problem

Solve the problem.

5 plastic bottles make 1 shirt.

How many shirts do 10 plastic bottles make?

_____ shirts

© Houghton Mifflin Harcourt Publishing Company · (c) ©Image Club Graphics; Eyewire/Getty Images

Sum It Up!

① Draw It!

Draw a picture of land pollution.
Draw a picture of water pollution.

land

water

② Match It!

Draw a line to match each word to the picture it tells about.

recycle   reduce   reuse

© Houghton Mifflin Harcourt Publishing Company

Name _____

Word Play

Use the words to complete the letter.

| pollution | reduce | reuse | recycle | conservation |

Dear Ben,

I just joined a club. We _____ paper so it can be made into new things. We _____ cans to make pencil holders. It is a good idea to shut off lights when we leave rooms. This helps _____ our use of resources. _____ is another way to protect our resources.

Soon we will clean up trash in the park. _____ could harm the living things there. Let's go to the park together!

Your Friend,
Ming

© Houghton Mifflin Harcourt Publishing Company

Apply Concepts

Write a word from the box to fill in the blanks.

| reduce | reuse | recycle |

Cause

I _____
a bottle as a
flower vase.

I _____ cans.

I turn off the
water when I
brush my teeth.

Effect

I make less trash.

The old cans are
used to make
new pots.

I _____
the amount of
water I use.

Take It Home!

Family Members: Work with your child to identify household items that can be recycled or reused. Find ways to reduce the use of resources in your home.

228

© Houghton Mifflin Harcourt Publishing Company

Vocabulary Review

Use the terms in the box to complete the sentences.

ocean
product
recycle

TEKS 1.1C

1. When you _____ paper, you use old paper to make new paper.

TEKS 1.7B

2. An _____ is a large body of salty water.

TEKS 1.7C

3. A brick is a _____ that is made from soil.

Science Concepts

Fill in the letter of the choice that best answers the question.

TEKS 1.2B, 1.7A

4. Nick investigates. He observes that one soil is smooth and one is lumpy. What property of the soil did Nick observe?

   Ⓐ color

   Ⓑ texture

   Ⓒ size of rock bits

TEKS 1.7B

5. Which body of water has land all around it? Identify it.

   Ⓐ lake

   Ⓑ river

   Ⓒ stream

© Houghton Mifflin Harcourt Publishing Company

6. How does the soil in this garden help to make useful products?

Ⓐ It helps to make statues.

Ⓑ It helps to make jewelry.

Ⓒ It helps grow food for people to eat.

7. What is silt made of?

Ⓐ large bits of rock

Ⓑ medium bits of rock

Ⓒ small bits of rock

8. Why are soils different colors?

Ⓐ They get different amounts of rain.

Ⓑ They have different materials in them.

Ⓒ They hold different amounts of water.

9. Water can help make useful products. Which of these products includes water?

Ⓐ

SHAMPOO

Ⓑ

Ⓒ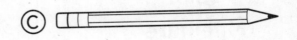

© Houghton Mifflin Harcourt Publishing Company

TEKS 1.2C, 1.7A

10. Tim is using tools to separate soil into parts. Which tool could he use?

Ⓐ a balance

Ⓑ a sieve

Ⓒ a thermometer

TEKS 1.2C, 1.4A, 1.7A

11. Jill wants to observe the size of the bits in this soil. Which tool should she use?

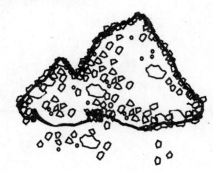

Ⓐ a balance

Ⓑ a hand lens

Ⓒ a thermometer

TEKS 1.1C

12. This bird feeder is made from a plastic milk jug.

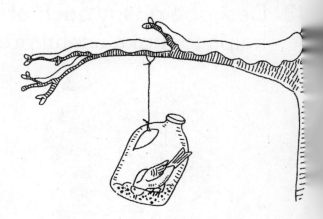

Which word describes how the milk jug is being used?

Ⓐ recycle

Ⓑ reduce

Ⓒ reuse

© Houghton Mifflin Harcourt Publishing Company

nquiry and the Big Idea

Write the answers to these questions.

3. Describe a way each of these natural resources helps to make useful products.

a.

_____

b.

_____

_____

14. Describe how you can reuse something at home or at school. How does learning to reuse things help the environment?

_____

_____

© Houghton Mifflin Harcourt Publishing Company

Weather and Seasons

winter weather

Big Idea

Weather changes from day to day and from season to season. You can use different tools to measure weather.

TEKS 1.2A, 1.2B, 1.2D, 1.3A, 1.3B, 1.3C, 1.8A, 1.8C, 1.8D

I Wonder Why

Icicles form in winter. Why?
Turn the page to find out.

© Houghton Mifflin Harcourt Publishing Company   (bg) ©Carol/Koh/Corbis; (inset) ©John Sylvester/Alamy; (border) ©Nise/Age Fotostock

Here's Why Winter weather can be cold. Liquid water can freeze into a solid during winter.

In this unit, you will explore this Big Idea, the Essential Questions, and the Investigations on the Inquiry Flipchart.

Levels of Inquiry Key ■ DIRECTED ■ GUIDED ■ INDEPENDENT

Track Your Progress

Big Idea Weather changes from day to day and from season to season. You can use different tools to measure weather.

Essential Questions

Lesson 1 What Is Weather? 235
Inquiry Flipchart p. 32—Hot or Cold?/Windsock Workshop

Inquiry Lesson 2 What Can We Observe About Weather? 247
Inquiry Flipchart p. 33—What Can We Observe About Weather?

👥 **People in Science:** June Bacon-Bercey. 251

Lesson 3 What Are Seasons? 253
Inquiry Flipchart p. 34—Keeping Warm/Turn Over a New Leaf

S.T.E.M. Engineering and Technology: Weather Wisdom. 265
Inquiry Flipchart p. 35—Build It: Rain Gauge

Unit 6 Review 267

Now I Get the Big Idea!

Science Notebook

Before you begin each lesson, be sure to write your thoughts about the Essential Question.

© Houghton Mifflin Harcourt Publishing Company (bg) ©Carol Kohl/Corbis; (inset) ©John Sylvester/Alamy; (border) ©NDisc/Age Fotostock

TEKS **1.8A** record weather information, including relative temperature, such as hot or cold, clear or cloudy, calm or windy, and rainy or icy **1.8D** demonstrate that air is all around us and observe that wind is moving air

Essential Question

What Is Weather?

Engage Your Brain!

Find the answer to the question in the lesson.

Rainbows usually follow rainy weather. Which tool could you use to measure rainfall?

_____

Active Reading

Lesson Vocabulary

1 Preview the lesson.

2 Write the 4 vocabulary terms here.

_____   _____

_____   _____

© Houghton Mifflin Harcourt Publishing Company (bg) ©Radius Images/Corbis

Weather Watch

Look outside. Is it sunny? Is the air warm or cool? Are there any clouds? Do you feel any wind? **Wind** is air that moves.

Weather is what the air outside is like. Weather may change during the day. It may also change from day to day and from month to month.

Active Reading

A detail is a fact about a main idea. Draw one line under a detail. Draw an arrow to the main idea the detail tells about.

Is it cloudy or sunny?

Is it windy or calm?

© Houghton Mifflin Harcourt Publishing Company (bl) ©Philip Coblentz/Brand X/Corbis; (br) ©Stephanie Friedman/Alamy

Is it rainy or icy?

Is it hot or cold?

Is it cloudy or clear?

▶ **Record weather information. Read the captions. Circle the word that tells about the weather in each picture.**

© Houghton Mifflin Harcourt Publishing Company (tl) ©Ian Sanderson/Getty Images; (c) ©Darby Sawchuk/Alamy; (tr) ©Oxford Picture Library/Alamy

Measure It!

You can use tools to measure weather. A thermometer is a tool that measures temperature. **Temperature** is the measure of how hot or cold something is. Temperature is measured in degrees.

Active Reading

Find the sentence that tells the meaning of **temperature**. Draw a line under the sentence.

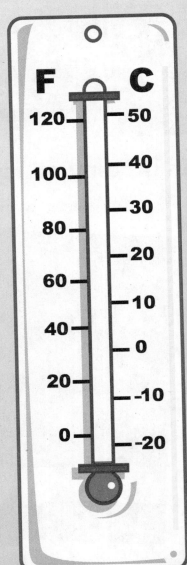

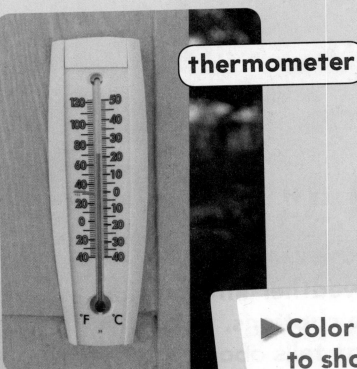

thermometer

► Color the thermometer to show 80 °F.

© Houghton Mifflin Harcourt Publishing Company

Rain, snow, sleet, and hail are
forms of water that fall from the sky.
A rain gauge is a tool that measures
how much water falls.

rain gauge

▶ Color the rain gauge to show
that three inches of rain fell.

© Houghton Mifflin Harcourt Publishing Company

Catch the Wind

Air moves all around us. How do you know which way it moves? How do you know how fast it moves? You can use tools to observe the wind. A **windsock** is a tool that shows the direction of the wind.

It is a windy day. The windsock is filled with air.

© Houghton Mifflin Harcourt Publishing Company (l) Pierre BRYE/Alamy

This tool measures wind speed.

The wind vane shows the direction the wind is coming from.

▶ Observe that wind is moving air. What makes the windsock move?

_____

_____

© Houghton Mifflin Harcourt Publishing Company (t) ©matthiasengelien.com/Alamy Images; (b) ©Raine Vara/Alamy Images

Predict It!

Scientists observe and track weather over time. They look for changes in weather. They use tools to learn what the weather may be. Scientists use what they learn to make a weather report. A weather report helps people. They can get ready for the coming weather.

weather satellite

Do the Math!

Compare Numbers

Monday

50 °F

Tuesday

40 °F

Wednesday

45 °F

© Houghton Mifflin Harcourt Publishing Company   (cr) ©European Space Agency/AOES Medialab/Photo Researchers, Inc.

We use these tools to observe and track weather.

weather station

weather balloon

Look at the temperatures on the left.

Write one of them in the empty box below.

Write >, <, or = to compare the two numbers.

45 °F		_____ °F

© Houghton Mifflin Harcourt Publishing Company (tl) ©Larry Landolfi/Photo Researchers, Inc.; (tr) ©David R. Frazier/Photo Researchers, Inc.

Sum It Up!

① Draw It!

Look outside. Draw to record the weather you observe.

② Circle It!

Circle the picture that shows wind is moving air.

③ Match It!

Match the words to the pictures.

rain gauge

thermometer

© Houghton Mifflin Harcourt Publishing Company

Name _____

Word Play

Unscramble the word to complete each sentence.

wind	weather	temperature	windsock

1. trwahee   _ _ _ _ _ _ _ is what the air outside is like.

2. ueeratpmret   _ _ _ _ _ _ _ _ _ _ _ is how hot or cold something is.

3. ndiw   Air that moves is called _ _ _ _.

4. diwnoskc   A _ _ _ _ _ _ _ _ is a tool that shows the direction of the wind.

© Houghton Mifflin Harcourt Publishing Company

Apply Concepts

Write a word from the box to fill in the blanks.

cold	windy	sunny	hot

Observation	Inference
Children are swimming in the lake.	The day is _____.
Air is moving the trees back and forth.	The day is _____.
People are wearing warm coats.	The day is _____.
People are wearing sunglasses.	The day is _____.

Take It Home!

Family Members: Look up the weather forecast with your child. Together, predict the weather for the coming week. Have your child record the weather for the week.

© Houghton Mifflin Harcourt Publishing Company

Inquiry Flipchart p. 33

TEKS **1.2A** ask questions about … events observed in the natural world **1.2B** plan and conduct simple descripti investigations … **1.2D** record and organize data using pictures, numbers, a words **1.3B** make predictions based on observable patterns **1.8A** record weathe information, including relative temperatu such as hot or cold, clear or cloudy, calm windy, and rainy or icy

Name _____

Essential Question

What Can We Observe About Weather?

Set a Purpose

Tell what you want to find out.

_____

_____

Think About the Procedure

1 When will you observe the weather?

_____

_____

2 What will you observe?

_____

_____

© Houghton Mifflin Harcourt Publishing Company

Record Your Data

Record the weather. Glue picture cards into the chart.

Weather This Week

Monday	Tuesday	Wednesday	Thursday	Friday

Draw Conclusions

How is the weather alike from day to day?
How is the weather different from day to day?

_____

_____

How did you make your prediction?

_____

Ask More Questions

What other questions could you ask about the weather?

_____

© Houghton Mifflin Harcourt Publishing Company

Picture Cards
Cut out the weather cards.

clear	clear	clear	clear	clear
cloudy	cloudy	cloudy	cloudy	cloudy
rainy	rainy	rainy	rainy	rainy
icy	icy	icy	icy	icy
hot	hot	hot	hot	hot
cold	cold	cold	cold	cold
windy	windy	windy	windy	windy
calm	calm	calm	calm	calm

© Houghton Mifflin Harcourt Publishing Company

4

Things to Know About

June Bacon-Bercey

1 June Bacon-Bercey is a meteorologist.

2 She was the first female meteorologist on television.

3 She won money, which she used to help other women become meteorologists.

4 She enjoys teaching.

© Houghton Mifflin Harcourt Publishing Company (bkgd) ©Ralph H Wetmore II/Getty Images

Word Whiz

▶ **Learn weather words. Find the words in the word search below. Draw a circle around each word you find.**

tornado	hurricane	lightning	thunder	storm	blizzard

```
l  i  g  h  t  n  i  n  g  q
w  m  r  n  o  t  b  y  v  h
b  d  l  z  r  x  s  p  c  u
l  t  h  u  n  d  e  r  b  r
i  j  g  s  a  y  z  q  m  r
z  q  f  g  d  g  f  d  s  i
z  w  s  t  o  r  m  h  j  c
a  r  d  k  y  y  p  l  k  a
r  t  s  h  p  q  w  r  t  n
d  y  p  f  j  s  d  c  b  e
```

© Houghton Mifflin Harcourt Publishing Company

TEKS **1.3B** make predictions based on observable patterns **1.8C** identify characteristics of the seasons of the year and day and night

Essential Question

What Are Seasons?

🧠 Engage Your Brain!

Find the answer to the question in the lesson.

In which season do many trees have no leaves?

_____

Active Reading

Lesson Vocabulary

1 Preview the lesson.

2 Write the 2 vocabulary terms here.

_____   _____

© Houghton Mifflin Harcourt Publishing Company   (bg) ©Zena Elea/Alamy

Inquiry Flipchart   p. 34—Keeping Warm/Turn Over a New Leaf

Spring Into Spring

A **season** is a time of year. Spring, summer, fall, and winter are the four seasons. They form a repeating pattern.

The weather changes with each season. These changes form a weather pattern. A **weather pattern** is a change in the weather that repeats.

Active Reading

Find the sentence that tells the meaning of **season**. Draw a line under the sentence.

People plant flowers in spring.

© Houghton Mifflin Harcourt Publishing Company   (b) ©Dennis MacDonald/Alamy

In spring, the air warms. There may be many rainy days. Plants begin to grow. Trees grow new leaves. People can wear light jackets outside.

▶ **Identify what spring is like.**

_____

_____

Some animals have their young in spring.

© Houghton Mifflin Harcourt Publishing Company (inset) ©William Leaman/Alamy

Sunny Summer

Summer is the season that follows spring. In summer, the air can be hot. Some places may have storms. There are more hours of daylight than in spring.

Some plants grow fruit in summer. Young animals grow bigger. People dress to stay cool. They wear hats and sunglasses to keep safe from the sun.

▶ Draw an object on the adult that would keep him safe from the sun.

People canoe in summer.

© Houghton Mifflin Harcourt Publishing Company   (tc) ©Dennis MacDonald/Alamy

▶ **Draw to show how most trees look in summer.**

This hare's fur is brown in summer. The brown fur helps the hare hide.

© Houghton Mifflin Harcourt Publishing Company (inset) ©fmahatstock.com/Alamy

Fall Into Fall

Fall is the season that follows summer. The air gets cooler. There are fewer hours of daylight than in summer.

Some leaves change color and drop off the trees. Some animals move to warmer places. People wear jackets to stay warm.

Active Reading

A detail is a fact about a main idea. Draw one line under a detail. Draw an arrow to the main idea it tells about.

People rake leaves in fall.

© Houghton Mifflin Harcourt Publishing Company   (tc) ©Dennis MacDonald/Alamy

▶ Draw to show how some trees look in fall.

Some animals gather food to store in winter.

© Houghton Mifflin Harcourt Publishing Company (inset) ©Peter Arnold Inc./Alamy

Winter Weather

Winter is the season that follows fall. In some places, the air can be cold. It may even snow. Winter has the fewest hours of daylight.

Many trees lose their leaves in winter. Some animals grow more fur to keep warm. People wear warm coats outside. In a few months, it will be spring again.

▶ **Draw winter clothes on the person not dressed for the season.**

People play in the snow in winter.

© Houghton Mifflin Harcourt Publishing Company (bg) ©Dennis MacDonald/Alamy

▶ You can make predictions based on patterns you have observed. The seasons form a pattern. Predict which season comes after winter.

_____

The hare's fur has turned white. The hare can hide in the snow.

© Houghton Mifflin Harcourt Publishing Company (inset) ©Ocean/Corbis

Sum It Up!

① Solve It!

Write the word that solves the riddle.

I am a time when trees have lots of leaves, or no leaves at all.
I am winter, spring, summer, or fall.
I am a _____ .

② Draw It!

Draw an activity you can do in spring.

③ Match It!

Match each word to the picture it tells about.

summer   winter   fall

© Houghton Mifflin Harcourt Publishing Company

Brain Check

Name _____

Word Play

Use the words below to complete the puzzle.

season	weather pattern	winter
spring	summer	fall

Across

1. the season that follows fall

2. the season that follows spring

3. the season that follows summer

4. a time of year

Down

5. the season that follows winter

6. a change in the weather that repeats

© Houghton Mifflin Harcourt Publishing Company

Apply Concepts

Identify what the seasons are like. Cross out the things that do **not** belong in each picture.

Family Members: Plan out family activities for the four seasons. Discuss with your child how the weather in each season affects what you do and what you wear.

Take It Home!

© Houghton Mifflin Harcourt Publishing Company

TEKS **1.3A** identify and explain a problem such as finding a home for a classroom pet and propose a solution in his/her own words **1.4A** collect and compare information using tools, ... including weather instruments ... **1.8A** record weather information ...

S.T.E.M.

Engineering and Technology

Weather Wisdom

Weather Tools

People wanted to observe and record weather. They designed tools to help them. The tools have changed and improved over time.

A thermometer measures temperature.

A weather satellite records weather from space.

A wind vane tells the direction of the wind.

A weather plane records weather from the sky.

© Houghton Mifflin Harcourt Publishing Company (cl) ©Simon Belcher/Alamy; (cr) ©Erik Simonsen/Getty Images; (bl) ©Jim Edds/Jim Reed Photography/Corbis; (br) ©Kevin R. Morris/Corbis

Weather Tool Timeline

Use the timeline to answer the questions.

1 Which is the oldest weather tool? Circle it.

2 Which is the newest weather tool?
Draw a box around it.

3 Which tool came after the thermometer?
Draw an X over it.

Build On It!

Design and build your own rain gauge. Complete **Build It: Rain Gauge** on the Inquiry Flipchart.

Name _____

Vocabulary Review

Use the terms in the box to complete the sentences.

season
temperature
weather

TEKS 1.8A

1. In spring, you can record the
   _____ as warm and rainy.

TEKS 1.3B

2. Winter is the _____ that comes after fall.

TEKS 1.8A

3. When you measure _____, you tell how hot or cold something is.

Science Concepts

Fill in the letter of the choice that best answers the question.

TEKS 1.4A, 1.8A

4. What tool can you use to collect and record the temperature each day?
   Ⓐ a rain gauge
   Ⓑ a thermometer
   Ⓒ a windsock

TEKS 1.3B, 1.8A

5. You see dark clouds in the sky. What kind of weather is **most likely** coming?
   Ⓐ cold weather
   Ⓑ rainy weather
   Ⓒ sunny weather

© Houghton Mifflin Harcourt Publishing Company

. In which season was this young lamb **most likely** born?

Ⓐ fall

Ⓑ spring

Ⓒ summer

TEKS 1.8C

7. The Han family is ice skating outside. They are wearing heavy jackets. Which season is it?

Ⓐ spring

Ⓑ summer

Ⓒ winter

TEKS 1.8C

8. How is fall **different** from spring?

Ⓐ Fall is a season.

Ⓑ People may wear jackets in spring.

Ⓒ Many trees lose their leaves in fall.

TEKS 1.8A

9. Pablo's rain gauge is full. There are dark clouds in the sky. He records what he observes. What does this tell you about the weather?

Ⓐ It is calm.

Ⓑ It is clear.

Ⓒ It is rainy.

© Houghton Mifflin Harcourt Publishing Company

10. Look at this picture. What is the weather like?

Ⓐ calm and cold
Ⓑ cold and snowy
Ⓒ windy and warm

11. Pradeep shows that air is all around us by using a windsock. What can he observe and record?

Ⓐ the direction of the wind
Ⓑ the temperature of the air
Ⓒ the speed of the wind

12. Look at what the children are doing.

Which season is it?
Ⓐ fall
Ⓑ winter
Ⓒ summer

© Houghton Mifflin Harcourt Publishing Company

Inquiry and the Big Idea
Write the answers to these questions:

TEKS 1.8A

13. Look at the picture.

a. Record what the weather is like.

_____

b. What might you wear on a day like this?

_____

c. What might you do on a day like this?

_____

TEKS 1.3B, 1.8C

14. Look at the tree.

a. Identify the season. Tell how you know which season it is.

_____

_____

b. Predict which season comes next.

_____

© Houghton Mifflin Harcourt Publishing Company

© Houghton Mifflin Harcourt Publishing Company (bg) ©Ted J. Clutter/Photo Researchers, Inc.; (inset) ©NASA; (border) ©DiscoAge Fotostock

UNIT 7
Objects in the Sky

moon in the nighttime sky

Big Idea

Many objects can be seen in the sky. The appearance of these objects can change.

TEKS 1.2A, 1.2B, 1.2D, 1.3A, 1.3B, 1.3C, 1.4A, 1.4B, 1.8B, 1.8C

I Wonder Why

The moon looks lit in the nighttime sky. Why?
Turn the page to find out.

Here's Why The moon reflects light from the sun. This makes it look lit at nighttime.

In this unit, you will explore this Big Idea, the Essential Questions, and the Investigations on the Inquiry Flipchart.

Levels of Inquiry Key ■ DIRECTED ■ GUIDED ■ INDEPENDENT

Track Your Progress

Big Idea Many objects can be seen in the sky. The appearance of these objects can change.

Essential Questions

Lesson 1 What Can We See in the Sky?............ 273
Inquiry Flipchart p. 36—High in the Sky/Star Fun

People in Science: Galileo Galilei 283

Lesson 2 How Does the Sky Seem to Change? 285
Inquiry Flipchart p. 37—Cloud Time/Moon and Stars Calendar

Inquiry Lesson 3 How Does the Sun Seem to Move? 295
Inquiry Flipchart p. 38—How Does the Sun Seem to Move?

S.T.E.M. Engineering and Technology: See the Light.... 297
Inquiry Flipchart p. 39—Design It: Lights for a Park

Unit 7 Review 299

Now I Get the Big Idea!

Science Notebook

Before you begin each lesson, be sure to write your thoughts about the Essential Question.

© Houghton Mifflin Harcourt Publishing Company (tl) ©Ted J. Clutter/Photo Researchers, Inc.; (bkgd) ©NDisc/Age Fotostock

Essential Question

What Can We See in the Sky?

Engage Your Brain!

Find the answer to the question in the lesson.

When can you see the moon?

_____

Active Reading

Lesson Vocabulary

1 Preview the lesson.

2 Write the 5 vocabulary terms here.

_____ _____

_____ _____

_____

© Houghton Mifflin Harcourt Publishing Company (bkgd) ©Chuck Pefley/Getty Images

Good Morning, Sunshine

sun

Look up! You can see many things in the daytime sky. You can see the sun. The **sun** is the star closest to Earth. A **star** is an object in the sky. It gives off its own light. The sun gives light and heat to Earth. It warms Earth's land, air, and water.

You may also see clouds in the daytime sky. Sometimes, you can even see the moon.

Active Reading

The main idea is the most important idea about something. Draw two lines under the main idea.

clouds

© Houghton Mifflin Harcourt Publishing Company   (bkgd) ©Thomas Northcut/Getty Images

► Look out your window. Identify what the daytime sky looks like. Draw what you see.

© Houghton Mifflin Harcourt Publishing Company (bkgd) ©Thomas Northcut/Getty Images

Good Night, Sky

moon

You can identify what the nighttime sky looks like. You may see the moon. The **moon** is a large sphere, or ball of rock. It does not give off its own light. You may also see clouds at night.

Active Reading

Draw one line under a detail. Draw an arrow to the main idea it tells about.

You may see stars in the nighttime sky. There are too many stars to count. They are not evenly spaced in the sky.

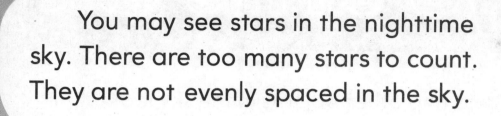

star

Do the Math!

Compare Solid Shapes

Many objects in the sky are spheres. A sphere is a round ball. The moon is a sphere. So is the sun. Color the spheres below.

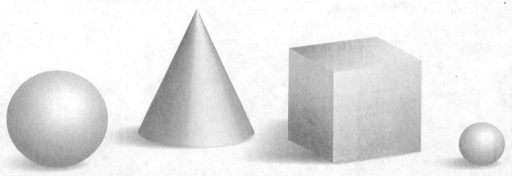

Eye on the Sky

Stars and other objects in the sky look small. We can magnify them to see them better. **Magnify** means to make something look bigger. A **telescope** is a tool that helps us magnify things in the sky.

© Houghton Mifflin Harcourt Publishing Company (boy) ©Charles C. Place

▶ **Which picture shows the moon through a telescope? Mark an X on it.**

telescope

Both pictures show the moon.

© Houghton Mifflin Harcourt Publishing Company (t) © R. Creation/Getty Images; (b) © Avalon Imaging / Alamy

Sum It Up!

1 Solve It!

Solve the riddle.

I am a tool. I make things look bigger. You can use me to observe things in the sky.
What am I?

_____

2 Circle It!

Circle true or false.

Stars are evenly spaced in the sky.

true   false

Stars give off their own light.

true   false

3 Draw It!

Draw what you can see in the sky at both times.

daytime	nighttime

© Houghton Mifflin Harcourt Publishing Company

Name _____

Word Play

Unscramble the letters to complete each sentence.

> sun   star   telescope   magnify   moon

omon   The ___ ___ ___ ___ is a large ball of rock.

tasr   A ___ ___ ___ ___ gives off its own light.

eletopsce   A ___ ___ ___ ___ ___ ___ ___ ___ ___ is a tool for making things look bigger.

usn   The ___ ___ ___ is the star we see in the day.

fimgany   To ___ ___ ___ ___ ___ ___ ___ is to make things look bigger.

© Houghton Mifflin Harcourt Publishing Company

Apply Concepts

1 Identify what the daytime and nighttime sky look like. Fill in the diagram to compare. Use the words below.

| sun | stars | clouds | moon |

daytime sky   both   nighttime sky

2 Draw a nighttime sky full of stars.

Family Members: Identify what the daytime and nighttime sky looks like with your child. Have your child explain how they are the same and different.

Take It Home!

© Houghton Mifflin Harcourt Publishing Company

4

Things to Know About

Galileo Galilei

1 Galileo lived in Italy more than 400 years ago.

2 His telescope made objects look 20 times bigger.

3 He discovered sunspots on the sun.

4 He found out that the planet Jupiter has four moons.

© Houghton Mifflin Harcourt Publishing Company (bkg) ©Ian Mckinnell/Getty Images

This Leads to That

Galileo used his telescope to observe the sun and planets.

He proved that Earth moves around the sun.

▶ **People used to think that the sun moved around Earth. Galileo proved this was wrong. Why is this important?**

_____

_____

_____

© Houghton Mifflin Harcourt Publishing Company (bkg) ©Stocktrek/Getty Images; (t) ©Gianni Tortoli/Photo Researchers, Inc.

TEKS **1.3B** make predictions based on observable patterns **1.8B** observe and record changes in the appearance of objects in the sky such as clouds, the Moon, and stars, including the Sun

Essential Question

How Does the Sky Seem to Change?

🧠 Engage Your Brain!

Find the answer to the question in the lesson.

Why does the sun seem to move across the sky?

Earth _____ .

Active Reading

Lesson Vocabulary

1 Preview the lesson.

2 Write the 2 vocabulary terms here.

_____

© Houghton Mifflin Harcourt Publishing Company (bg) ©David Hanby/Getty Images

Hello, Shadow

Each day, Earth turns all the way around. It makes the sun seem to move across the sky.

In the morning and late afternoon the sun seems low in the sky. It seems high at noon. This is a pattern that repeats each day as Earth turns.

Active Reading

The main idea is the most important idea about something. Draw two lines under the main idea.

morning

Houghton Mifflin Harcourt Publishing Company · (bkgd) ©Thomas Northcut/Getty Images

Light from the sun makes shadows. A **shadow** is a dark place made where an object blocks light. Shadows change as Earth moves. The sun's light shines on objects from different directions as the day goes on. Shadows change in size during the day. They change position, too.

▶ **Observe and record how the sun seems to change during the day.**

_____

_____

noon

afternoon

© Houghton Mifflin Harcourt Publishing Company (bkgd) ©Thomas Northcut/Getty Images

Just a Phase

Now it is night. You may see stars. You may see the moon. The moon is a huge ball of rock. It does not give off its own light. The moon reflects light from the sun.

Active Reading

A detail is a fact about a main idea. Draw one line under a detail. Draw an arrow to the main idea it tells about.

new moon

first quarter moon

© Houghton Mifflin Harcourt Publishing Company (bkg) ©Getty Images/PhotoDisc/Don Farrall

The moon moves across the sky. Its shape seems to change. The **phases**, or shapes you see, change as the moon moves. The changes follow a repeating pattern. It lasts about a month.

▶ Observe the full moon below. Predict what the moon's phase will be in about a month. Record it.

_____

full moon

third quarter moon

© Houghton Mifflin Harcourt Publishing Company   (b,cr) ©Getty Images/PhotoDisc/Don Farrall

Cloudy Day, Starry Night

You can see stars in the nighttime sky. Stars give off light. You see different stars in each season.

You can see clouds in both the daytime and nighttime sky. Clouds change shape from day to day.

You may see these stars in summer.

You may see these stars in winter.

© Houghton Mifflin Harcourt Publishing Company   (bl) ©Photo Network/Alamy; (br) ©Galaxy Picture Library/Alamy; (bg) ©Wes Thompson/Corbis

These kinds of clouds may bring rain.

These kinds of clouds can be seen on a sunny day.

▶ **Observe the clouds in the pictures. Record how they changed.**

_____

_____

_____

_____

© Houghton Mifflin Harcourt Publishing Company   (cl) ©W. Perry Conway/Corbis; (tr) ©Paul Souders/Corbis

Sum It Up!

① Solve It!

Write the word to solve the riddle.

I am fluffy or thin.
I am white or gray.
I come out on
some days and then
go away.
I am a _____.

② Draw It!

Draw the boy's shadow in the morning.

③ Mark It!

Cross out the picture of the full moon. Put a box around the picture of the new moon.

© Houghton Mifflin Harcourt Publishing Company

Name _____

Word Play

Label each picture with a word from the box.
Match the word to its meaning.

sun	phases	shadow

_____

dark place made where an object blocks light

_____

shapes you see of the moon

_____

brightest object in the daytime sky

© Houghton Mifflin Harcourt Publishing Company

Apply Concepts

Write the words that tell more about each column. Each word may be used more than once.

sun   clouds   stars   moon

Daytime Sky	Nighttime Sky	Gives Off Its Own Light	Moves or Seems to Move
_____	_____	_____	_____
_____	_____	_____	_____
_____	_____		_____
			_____

Take It Home!

Family Members: Observe objects in the sky, such as the clouds, the moon, and the stars. Ask your child to describe how each of these objects seems to change.

© Houghton Mifflin Harcourt Publishing Company

TEKS **1.2A** ask questions about organisms, objects, and events observe the natural world **1.2B** plan and condu simple descriptive investigations . . . **1.** record and organize data using pictures numbers, and words **1.4A** collect and compare information using tools, includi . . . non-standard measuring items . . . **1.4B** measure and compare organisms and objects using non-standard units **1.8B** observe and record changes in the appearance of objects in the sky such as clouds, the Moon, and stars, including the Sun

Name _____

Essential Question

How Does the Sun Seem to Move?

Set a Purpose

Tell what you want to find out.

_____

_____

Think About the Procedure

1 When will you look at your shadow?

_____

_____

2 How will you know how your shadow changes?

_____

© Houghton Mifflin Harcourt Publishing Company

Record Your Data

Write the number of shoes in the chart. Compare them.

My Shadow's Length

Morning	Noon	Afternoon
_____ shoes long	_____ shoes long	_____ shoes long

Draw Conclusions

How did your shadow change from morning to noon?

_____

How did it change from noon to afternoon?

_____

Why do you think your shadow changed?

_____

_____

Ask More Questions

What other questions could you ask about how objects seem to move in the sky?

_____

© Houghton Mifflin Harcourt Publishing Company

TEKS 1.3A identify and explain a problem such as finding a home for a classroom pet and propose a solution in his/her own words

See the Light

Compare Flashlights

Lights help you see what you are doing. They help you get around at night. The lights in a building make it bright.

Flashlights can light up dark places. Flashlights work in different ways.

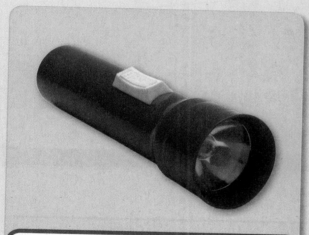

- uses a switch
- needs batteries
- lights up right away

- uses a hand crank
- does not need batteries
- takes time to light up

© Houghton Mifflin Harcourt Publishing Company

Bright Ideas

You have a problem. You need better lighting to read. How can you improve the lamp in your room? Draw your design. Tell how it works.

Build On It!

Design lights for a ballpark. Complete **Design It: Lights for a Park** on the Inquiry Flipchart.

© Houghton Mifflin Harcourt Publishing Company   (t) ©Peter Dazeley/Getty Images

Vocabulary Review
Use the terms in the box to complete the sentences.

phases
shadow
star

TEKS 1.8C

1. An object in the sky that gives off its own light is a

   _____.

TEKS 1.8B

2. A dark place made where an object blocks light is a

   _____.

TEKS 1.8B

3. The shapes of the moon you see as it moves are its

   _____.

Science Concepts
Fill in the letter of the choice that best answers the question.

TEKS 1.8C

4. You can see stars at night. How many stars are in the sky?
   - Ⓐ about 20
   - Ⓑ not enough to be counted
   - Ⓒ more than anyone can easily count

TEKS 1.8C

5. What objects can we see in the nighttime sky? Identify them.
   - Ⓐ the sun and clouds
   - Ⓑ the moon and stars
   - Ⓒ the sun and the moon

© Houghton Mifflin Harcourt Publishing Company

. Sophie observes how objects seem to change during the day. She records this in her notebook. Which objects did she observe?

(A) the moon and the stars

(B) the sun and the clouds

(C) the stars and the sun

7. Observe the picture of the moon. Which moon phase does it show?

(A) full moon

(B) new moon

(C) first quarter moon

8. Which happens because Earth turns?

(A) The sun warms Earth.

(B) The moon has phases.

(C) The sun seems to move across the sky.

9. How do stars look in the nighttime sky?

(A) They are scattered unevenly.

(B) They are set in a pattern of rings.

(C) They are set evenly across the sky.

© Houghton Mifflin Harcourt Publishing Company

10. Light from the sun makes shadows during the day. Which picture shows the flag's shadow at the end of the day?

Ⓐ The picture with the long shadow.

Ⓑ The picture with the short shadow.

Ⓒ Both pictures show the flag's shadow at the end of the day.

11. Yoon sees different stars on a winter night than he sees on a summer night. Why?

Ⓐ You can see stars only in the winter sky.

Ⓑ Clouds may block the stars in summer.

Ⓒ You can see different stars in different seasons.

12. Which object can you see in both the daytime and the nighttime sky?

Ⓐ

Ⓑ

Ⓒ

© Houghton Mifflin Harcourt Publishing Company

Inquiry and the Big Idea

Write the answers to these questions.

TEKS 1.2C, 1.8C

13. You want to get a closer look at the stars in the sky.

   a. What tool can help you see the stars better?

   _____

   b. How does this tool help you?

   _____

   _____

TEKS 1.8C

14. Compare and contrast the stars and the moon.

   a. What is one way they are the same?

   _____

   _____

   b. Name a way they are different.

   _____

   _____

   _____

© Houghton Mifflin Harcourt Publishing Company

UNIT 8
Living Things and Their Environments

Big Idea

Living and nonliving things are found in environments. A living thing lives in an environment that meets its needs.

TEKS 1.2A, 1.2B, 1.2D, 1.3A, 1.3C, 1.4A, 1.9A, 1.9B, 1.9C

deer in the forest

I Wonder Why

Deer live in the forest. Why?
Turn the page to find out.

© Houghton Mifflin Harcourt Publishing Company (c) ©Tom Tietz/Getty Images (inset) ©Robert Pickett/Corbis (border) ©NDisc/Age Fotostock

Here's Why A deer can meet its needs in the forest. It can find food, water, and shelter there.

In this unit, you will explore this Big Idea, the Essential Questions, and the Investigations on the Inquiry Flipchart.

Levels of Inquiry Key ■ DIRECTED ■ **GUIDED** ■ INDEPENDENT

Track Your Progress

Big Idea Living and nonliving things are found in environments. A living thing lives in an environment that meets its needs.

Essential Questions

Lesson 1 What Are Living and Nonliving Things? ... 305
Inquiry Flipchart p. 40—It's Alive!/Neighborhood Search

Lesson 2 Where Do Plants and Animals Live? 315
Inquiry Flipchart p. 41—Build an Aquarium/Working Together

Careers in Science: Forest Ranger 329

Inquiry Lesson 3 What Is a Terrarium? 331
Inquiry Flipchart p. 42—What Is a Terrarium?

S.T.E.M. **Engineering and Technology:**
A Place for Animals 333
Inquiry Flipchart p. 43—Design It: Butterfly Garden

Unit 8 Review 335

Now I Get the Big Idea!

Science Notebook

Before you begin each lesson, be sure to write your thoughts about the Essential Question.

© Houghton Mifflin Harcourt Publishing Company (t) ©Tom Tietz/Getty Images; (inset) ©Robert Pickett/Corbis; (border) ©NDisc/Age Fotostock

Essential Question

What Are Living and Nonliving Things?

Engage Your Brain!

Find the answer to the question in the lesson.

What do all living things need?

_____

Active Reading

Lesson Vocabulary

1 Preview the lesson.

2 Write the 4 vocabulary terms here.

_____ _____

_____ _____

© Houghton Mifflin Harcourt Publishing Company ©IDC/amanaimages/Corbis

Living It Up!

Living things are people, animals, and plants. They need food, water, air, and space to live. They grow and change. Living things **reproduce**. They make new living things like themselves.

_____

flowers

© Houghton Mifflin Harcourt Publishing Company

▶ Label the living things you see in the picture.

_____

_____

_____

_____

_____

groundhog

© Houghton Mifflin Harcourt Publishing Company

What's Nonliving?

Nonliving things do not need food, air, and water. They do not grow and change. What are some nonliving things? A rock is a nonliving thing. Air and water are nonliving things, too.

Active Reading

Find the sentences that tell the meaning of **nonliving things**. Draw a line under them.

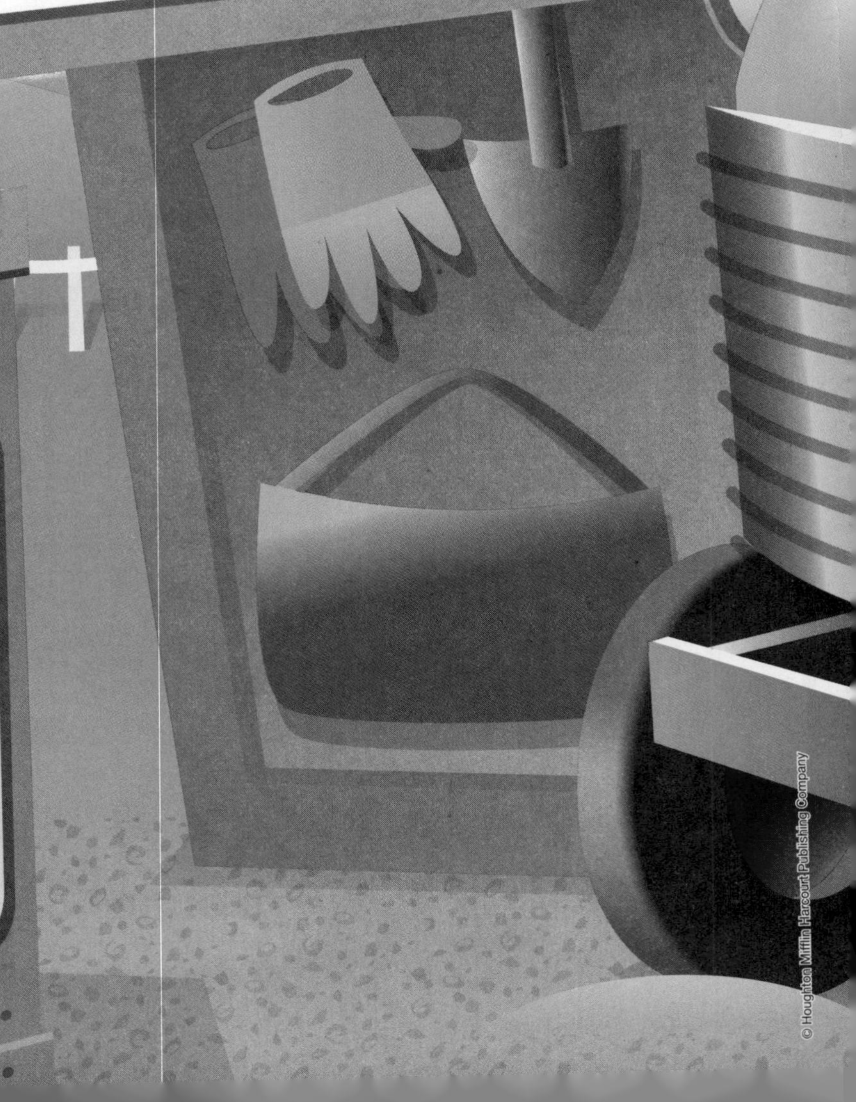

▶ List nonliving things you see.

_____

_____

_____

© Houghton Mifflin Harcourt Publishing Company

© Houghton Mifflin Harcourt Publishing Company

All Together

All the living and nonliving things in a place make up an **environment**. A farm is one environment. It has living and nonliving things.

Active Reading

The main idea is the most important idea about something. Draw two lines under the main idea.

© Houghton Mifflin Harcourt Publishing Company

► Living things have basic needs and can reproduce. Nonliving things do not. Classify things in a farm environment by these properties.

Living	Nonliving

© Houghton Mifflin Harcourt Publishing Company

Sum It Up!

① Choose It!

Classify each thing. Circle the living things. Draw an X on the nonliving things.

② Draw It!

Draw a living thing and a nonliving thing you might find in a park.

© Houghton Mifflin Harcourt Publishing Company

Name _____

Word Play

Classify parts of the picture as living or nonliving. Color the living things. Circle the nonliving things.

© Houghton Mifflin Harcourt Publishing Company

Apply Concepts

You can classify things as living or nonliving. Complete the chart to show how the groups are different.

Living Things	Nonliving Things
① grow and change	do not grow and change
② _____	do not reproduce
③ need air	do not need _____
④ need _____	do not need water
⑤ need food	do not need _____

Look around your environment. Name one living thing and one nonliving thing.

Living Thing	Nonliving Thing
⑥ _____	⑦ _____

Take It Home!

Family Members: Take a survey of your home with your child. Sort and classify the living things and the nonliving things you see.

© Houghton Mifflin Harcourt Publishing Company

TEKS **1.9B** analyze and record examples of interdependence found in various situations such as terrariums and aquariums or pet and caregiver **1.9C** gather evidence of interdependence among living organisms such as energy transfer through food chains and animals using plants for shelter

Essential Question

Where Do Plants and Animals Live?

Engage Your Brain!

Find the answer to the question in the lesson.

How is this rain forest animal using the tree?

_____

Active Reading

Lesson Vocabulary

1 Preview the lesson.

2 Write the 3 vocabulary terms here.

_____   _____

_____

Houghton Mifflin Harcourt Publishing Company © Marco Simoni/Photographer's Choice/Getty Images

All Around You

All the living and nonliving things around you make up your **environment**. A living thing lives in the environment that meets its needs.

Many animals need shelter. **Shelter** is a place where an animal can be safe.

Active Reading

Find the sentence that tells the meaning of **shelter**. Draw a line under the sentence.

The foxes are using this log for shelter.

© Houghton Mifflin Harcourt Publishing Company (bkg) ©Daniel J. Cox/Corbis

Salty Water

An ocean environment is a large body of salt water. Its top layer is home to many living things. Here, plants and other living things get the sunlight they need. Animals can find food.

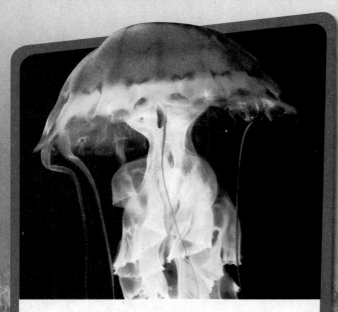

A jellyfish has body parts that help it catch its food.

Kelp lives in the ocean. Many animals eat it.

▶ **Why do many plants live in the top layer of the ocean?**

_____

_____

© Houghton Mifflin Harcourt Publishing Company (bkgd) ©Donald Tipton/Photo Researchers, Inc.; (cl) ©SMC Images/Photodisc/Getty Images; (cr) ©Hal Beral/Corbis

In a Rain Forest

A rain forest gets a lot of rain. The trees grow tall and block the sun. Many animals, such as birds and monkeys, use the tall trees for shelter. The shorter plants do not need much sunlight.

The rain forest provides everything this leopard needs to live.

▶ Draw a rain forest animal that uses trees or other plants for shelter.

© Houghton Mifflin Harcourt Publishing Company · (bkgd) © Frans Lanting/Corbis

Dry As a Bone

A desert environment gets little rain. Plants such as cactuses store water in their thick stems. Other plants store water in their leaves. In hot deserts, many animals hide during the day.

Desert plants and animals can live with little water.

desert hare

Gila monster

▶ **Draw a plant that stores water.**

A Joshua tree can be a shelter for small animals.

© Houghton Mifflin Harcourt Publishing Company. (bkgd) ©Michele Falzone/Photographer's Choice/Getty Images; (tr) ©Kenneth M. Highfill / Photo Researchers, Inc; (cr) ©Kennan Ward/Corbis

It's Cold Out Here!

A tundra is a very cold environment.
Plants grow close together near the ground.
Animals have thick fur to stay warm.

An Arctic fox's white fur helps it hide in the snow.

Arctic flowers

▶ **How does an Arctic fox's white fur help it in winter?**

_____

_____

_____

© Houghton Mifflin Harcourt Publishing Company (bkgd) ©Jim Zuckerman/Corbis; (inset) ©Chris Mattison/Frank Lane Picture Agency/Corbis

On the Prairie

A prairie environment is mostly dry. It has just a few kinds of trees and shrubs. Large animals eat the tall grasses. Smaller animals live in the grasses.

Active Reading

The main idea is the most important idea about something. Draw two lines under the main idea.

Some bison move to places with trees in the winter. The trees provide shelter from the cold.

coneflowers

prairie dogs

red-tailed hawk

© Houghton Mifflin Harcourt Publishing Company   (bkgd) © Mike Grandmaison/Corbis; (bl) © Martin Hughes-Jones / Alamy; (bc) © James Hager/Robert Harding World Imagery/Getty Images; (br) © Eric and David Hosking/Corbis

The Food Chain

All living things need energy from the sun. Plants use sunlight to make food. Then animals eat the plants. They get the energy they need from the plants.

A **food chain** shows how energy moves from plants to animals.

The grass uses sunlight to make food.

▶ Trace the arrows to show the order of the food chain.

© Houghton Mifflin Harcourt Publishing Company (tc) ©Fresh Start Images/Alamy; (inset) ©moodboard/Corbis

The cricket eats the grass.

The toad eats the cricket.

▶ How do living things depend on each other to get energy in this food chain?

_____

_____

_____

© Houghton Mifflin Harcourt Publishing Company (inset) ©Marvin Dembinsky Photo Associates/Alamy; (inset) ©Rick & Nora Bowers/Alamy

Caring for Pets

Think about some pets you know. Where do they get their food and water? Who gives them shelter? They need people.

A pet needs space to exercise and play. You need to keep the pet and its shelter clean.

▶ Analyze how a person helps care for a pet. Record your answer.

_____

_____

© Houghton Mifflin Harcourt Publishing Company (bkgd) Tanya Constantine/Getty Images

People need to take care of pets and keep them clean.

People need to give pets food.

This dog gets one cup of dog food in the morning and one cup of dog food at night.

How many cups of dog food does it get in one day?

1 cup in morning

+ 1 cup at night
_____

____ cups in one day

How many cups of dog food does it get in five days?

_____

© Houghton Mifflin Harcourt Publishing Company   (tl) ©Gen Nishino/Getty Images; (bl) ©Arco Images GmbH/Alamy

Sum It Up!

① Draw It!

Choose an environment. Draw a living thing meeting its needs there.

② Order It!

Show how energy moves among living things. Put the parts of the food chain in order.

_____   _____   _____

© Houghton Mifflin Harcourt Publishing Company

Name _____

Word Play

Read the journal entry. Fill in the blanks using words from the box.

shelter	food chain	environment

Dear Journal,

Today I took a field trip to Mulberry Forest. It is an _____ full of trees. Birds use the trees for _____.

The trees need sunlight to make food. The birds eat berries from the trees. The sun, the trees, and the birds are part of a _____. It was fun to learn about the forest.

Your Friend,
Swati

© Houghton Mifflin Harcourt Publishing Company

Apply Concepts

Write two details that go with the main idea.
Then answer the question.

Main Idea
A tundra is a cold environment.

Detail—Animals	Detail—Plants
_____	_____
_____	_____
_____	_____
_____	_____
_____	_____

What do all the living and nonliving things in a place

make up? _____

Family Members: Talk about your
environment with your child. Look for
examples of animals using plants for food
and for shelter.

Take It Home!

© Houghton Mifflin Harcourt Publishing Company

Ask a Forest Ranger

What does a forest ranger do?
I take care of forests.
I help keep plants and animals safe.
I also teach about nature and how to care for it.

How does a forest ranger help keep plants safe?
I teach people how to keep forest fires from starting.
I make sure no one cuts down trees.

How does a forest ranger help keep animals safe?
I make sure people do not feed them. I protect their homes by protecting the forest.

Now It's Your Turn!

▶ What question would you ask a forest ranger?

_____

_____

_____

© Houghton Mifflin Harcourt Publishing Company (bc) ©Mike Dobel/Alamy; (inset) ©David Young-Wolff/Alamy

Protect the Forest

▶ **Draw or write the answer to each question.**

1 Why are forest rangers important?

1
_____
_____
_____

2 What would you like best about being a forest ranger? What would you like least?

2
_____
_____
_____
_____

3 Suppose you are a forest ranger. Draw one animal or plant you help protect in the forest.

3

© Houghton Mifflin Harcourt Publishing Company   (bg) ©Mike Dobel/Alamy

TEKS **1.2A** ask questions about organisms, objects, and events observe in the natural world **1.2B** plan and conduct simple descriptive investigation such as ways objects move **1.2D** record and organize data using pictures numbers, and words **1.4A** collect and compare information using tools, includ . . . materials to support observations of habitats of organisms **1.9B** analyze an record examples of interdependence fou in various situations such as terrariums aquariums or pet and caregiver

Name _____

Essential Question

What Is a Terrarium?

Set a Purpose

Tell what you want to find out.

_____

_____

Think About the Procedure

❶ What do you put inside the bottle?

_____

_____

❷ What will you observe about the pill bugs?

_____

_____

© Houghton Mifflin Harcourt Publishing Company

Record Your Data

Write to record what you observed in the chart.

My Pill Bug Observations	
Day 1	
Day 2	
Day 3	
Day 4	
Day 5	

Draw Conclusions

Analyze your observations. How did the terrarium help you understand what animals need to live?

_____

_____

Ask More Questions

Compare your terrarium to other habitats. What other questions could you ask about observing habitats?

_____

_____

© Houghton Mifflin Harcourt Publishing Company

A Place for Animals

Keeping Animals Safe

People design and build safe places for animals. These places provide food, water, and shelter. People can help sick animals get well.

This animal doctor is checking on the health of the chimps.

These elephants are getting the food they need to live and grow.

These birds are getting water from the river.

© Houghton Mifflin Harcourt Publishing Company (br) ©Richard van Kesteren/Alamy; (tc) ©Penny Tweedie/Corbis; (bl) ©Simon Hathaway/Alamy

S.T.E.M.
continued

Map It!

This map shows a place designed for animals. People make sure the animals can meet their needs there. Use the map to find out how.

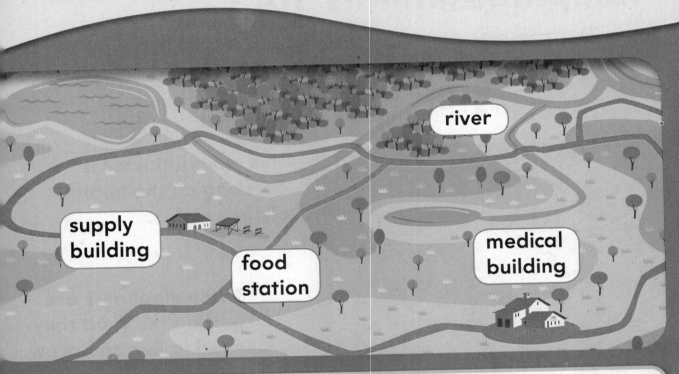

Circle where animals can get food.

Draw an X where animals can get water.

Draw a box around where sick animals can get well.

Build On It!

 Design a place for butterflies to live and grow. Complete **Design It: Butterfly Garden** on the Inquiry Flipchart.

© Houghton Mifflin Harcourt Publishing Company

Name _____

Vocabulary Review

Use the terms in the box to complete the sentences.

environment
reproduce
shelter

TEKS 1.9C

1. An animal might use a plant for

   _____.

TEKS 1.9B

2. All the living and nonliving things around you make up your

   _____.

TEKS 1.9A

3. When animals make new living things like themselves, they

   _____.

Science Concepts

Fill in the letter of the choice that best answers the question.

TEKS 1.9A

4. How are living things **different** from nonliving things?

   Ⓐ They may be large or small.

   Ⓑ They have needs and reproduce.

   Ⓒ They can be found in many places.

TEKS 1.9B

5. A kangaroo rat needs little water to live. It lives underground to stay cool. Which **best** meets its needs?

   Ⓐ a desert

   Ⓑ an ocean

   Ⓒ a tundra

© Houghton Mifflin Harcourt Publishing Company

6. Which of these has basic needs?

Ⓐ

Ⓑ

Ⓒ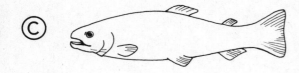

7. What kind of animal might live on the prairie?

Ⓐ an animal that eats grass

Ⓑ an animal that can live with little water

Ⓒ an animal that uses tall trees for shelter

8. Jamie is investigating the needs of animals. She observes the birds. Which need are these birds meeting?

Ⓐ air
Ⓑ food
Ⓒ water

9. How is this animal using the log?

Ⓐ for food
Ⓑ for shelter
Ⓒ for water

© Houghton Mifflin Harcourt Publishing Company

10. Which is **true** about an animal you keep as a pet?

Ⓐ It does not have basic needs.

Ⓑ It needs people to help it meet its needs.

Ⓒ It does not need shelter or food.

11. How might one living thing depend on another living thing in an ocean environment?

Ⓐ A shark might use a fish for food.

Ⓑ A bird might use a tree for shelter.

Ⓒ A cow might use grass for food.

12. Felix draws this food chain in his science notebook.

What does this food chain show?

Ⓐ The caterpillar uses the frog for food.

Ⓑ The frog uses the leaf for food.

Ⓒ The frog uses the caterpillar for food.

© Houghton Mifflin Harcourt Publishing Company

Inquiry and the Big Idea

Write the answers to these questions.

TEKS 1.9A, 1.9C

13. Look at this deer.

a. What need is this deer meeting?

_____

b. Name two other needs the deer has.

_____

TEKS 1.9B, 1.9C

14. You can gather evidence of how living things depend on each other. You can make a terrarium. Put pill bugs in a jar with soil, damp leaves, and a few rotten vegetables. After a few days, you see that most of the vegetables are gone. You see pill bugs hiding under the damp leaves.

Analyze and record how the bugs need other things in the terrarium.

_____

_____

_____

© Houghton Mifflin Harcourt Publishing Company

Animals

© Houghton Mifflin Harcourt Publishing Company (bkgd) ©Arthur Morris/Corbis; (inset) ©Dan Guravich/Corbis; (border) ©NDisc/Age Fotostock

Big Idea

Animals have adaptations that help them survive. Animals have different life cycles.

adult spoonbill

TEKS 1.2A, 1.2B, 1.2D, 1.3A, 1.3C, 1.10A, 1.10C, 1.10D

I Wonder How

Life cycles of animals can be different. How?
Turn the page to find out.

Here's How Some animals are born live. Some hatch from eggs. Some young look like their parents. Others do not.

In this unit, you will explore this Big Idea, the Essential Questions, and the Investigations on the Inquiry Flipchart.

Levels of Inquiry Key ■ DIRECTED ■ GUIDED ■ INDEPENDENT

Track Your Progress

Big Idea Animals have adaptations that help them survive. Animals have different life cycles.

Essential Questions

✓ **Lesson 1 How Do Animals Differ?** 341
Inquiry Flipchart p. 44—Animals Adapt/Picture Walk Safari

Inquiry Lesson 2 How Can We Group Animals? 353
Inquiry Flipchart p. 45—How Can We Group Animals?

S.T.E.M. Engineering and Technology: On the Farm 357
Inquiry Flipchart p. 46—Design It: Guard the Lettuce!

Lesson 3 What Are Some Animal Life Cycles? 359
Inquiry Flipchart p. 47—Where's the Caterpillar?/What's My Life Cycle?

Careers in Science: Zoo Keeper 371

Unit 9 Review 373

Now I Get the Big Idea!

Science Notebook

Before you begin each lesson, be sure to write your thoughts about the Essential Question.

© Houghton Mifflin Harcourt Publishing Company (bkgrd) ©Arthur Morris/Corbis (inset) ©Dan Guravich/Corbis (border) ©DigitalVue/Fotostock

Essential Question

How Do Animals Differe?

🧠 Engage Your Brain!

Find the answer to the question in the lesson.

This insect looks like a twig. How does this allow it to stay safe?

_____

Active Reading

Lesson Vocabulary

1 Preview the lesson.

2 Write the vocabulary term here.

_____

© Houghton Mifflin Harcourt Publishing Company ©Joel Sartore/National Geographic/Getty Images

Adaptable Animals

Animals have different body parts and behaviors. These are adaptations. An **adaptation** is a body part or behavior that helps a living thing survive. Adaptations allow animals to live where they do.

Active Reading

Find the sentence that tells the meaning of **adaptation.** Draw a line under the sentence.

Thick body fat lets the walrus live in a cold place.

© Houghton Mifflin Harcourt Publishing Company ©Vladimir Seliverstov/arfasster

Fish live in water.
They use gills to take in
oxygen from the water.

© Houghton Mifflin Harcourt Publishing Company ©Digital Vision/Getty Images

▶ What allows a
walrus to live in a
cold place?

_____

_____

The elephant lives in a hot place.
Big ears keep it cool.

Move It!

Adaptations allow animals to move. Animals use different body parts to move in different ways. What body parts are these animals using to move?

Monkeys use arms and legs to climb and swing.

Frogs use strong back legs to jump.

© Houghton Mifflin Harcourt Publishing Company; imagebroker/Alamy; ©Oxford Scientific/Getty Images; ©Peter Weimann/Picture Press/Getty Images

Fish use fins to swim.

Birds use wings to fly.

▶ **Look at the pictures. Circle the body parts a bird uses to fly. Put an X on the body parts a frog uses to jump.**

Cheetahs use strong legs to run fast.

© Houghton Mifflin Harcourt Publishing Company ©Juergen and Christin Sohns/Picture Press/Getty Images; ©MedioImages/Getty Images

Time to Eat

Adaptations allow animals to eat.
Animals that eat meat have sharp teeth.
Animals that eat plants have flat teeth.
Birds do not have teeth. You can tell what
a bird eats by the shape of its beak.

Active Reading

The main idea is the most important idea about
something. Draw two lines under the main idea.

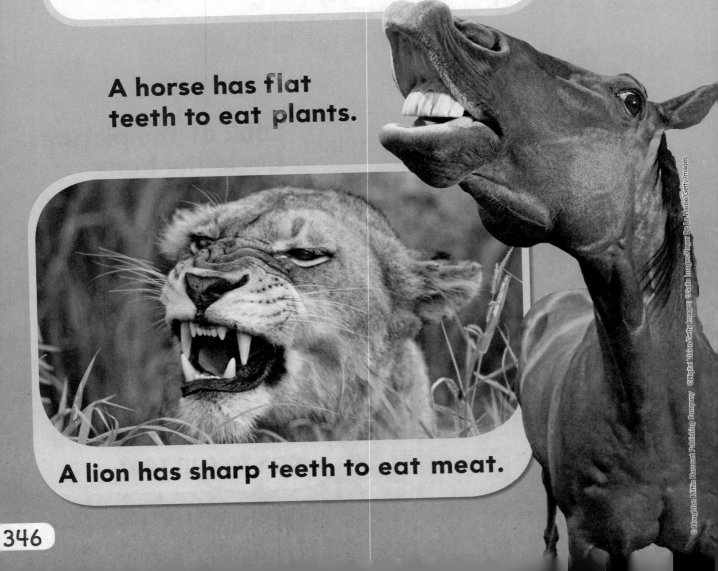

A horse has flat
teeth to eat plants.

A lion has sharp teeth to eat meat.

This bird has a short, rounded beak to eat seeds.

This bird has a long beak to eat insects.

Do the Math!

Solve a Word Problem

Solve the problem.

An adult horse has 20 teeth. An adult rabbit has 14 teeth.

How many more teeth does the horse have?

_____ – _____ = _____ more teeth

© Houghton Mifflin Harcourt Publishing Company ©Helen Williams/Photo Researchers; ©John Devries/Photo Researchers/Getty Images; ©John Devries/Photo Researchers, Inc.

Hide Me!

Adaptations allow animals to hunt. They can keep animals safe, too. Adaptations allow many animals to hide. Their colors and shapes let them blend in. You may not see the animals at all!

Color and shape allow this animal to hide.

©Houghton Mifflin Harcourt Publishing Company ©Mark Conlin/Oxford Scientific/Getty Images

▶ Look at the pictures. Circle each animal hiding.

Brown feathers let the owl hide in the tree.

Rough skin lets the frog hide on the branch.

Stripes hide the tiger in tall grass.

© Houghton Mifflin Harcourt Publishing Company ©WILDLIFE GmbH/Alamy Images; ©Michelle Gilders/Alamy Images; ©Steve Winter/National Geographic/Getty Images

Sum It Up!

① Circle It!

Circle the animal that could live here.

a seal

a lizard

a parrot

② Match It!

Match the animal with the kind of teeth it has.

sharp teeth

flat teeth

③ Write It!

Write the name of the body part the rabbit uses to move.

_____

© Houghton Mifflin Harcourt Publishing Company

Name _____

Word Play

Read each riddle. Then write the word that answers it.

| teeth | adaptation |

That's me up there in the sky.
I have big wings.
They let me fly.
What do you call these wings
of mine?

_____

I have parts that allow me to eat.
They are very sharp.
They tear up meat.
What parts are these?

_____

© Houghton Mifflin Harcourt Publishing Company

Apply Concepts

Read each main idea. Add details that tell which body parts animals may use.

Adaptations

Main Idea	Details
Where Animals Live	_____ _____
How Animals Move	_____ _____
How Animals Eat	_____ _____

Take It Home!

Family Members: Work with your child to investigate how animals such as pets and local wildlife use their body parts to eat, move, and live where they do.

© Houghton Mifflin Harcourt Publishing Company

TEKS **1.2A** ask questions about organisms, objects, and events **1.2B** plan and conduct simple descriptive investigations such as ways objects mov **1.2D** record and organize data using pictures, numbers, and words **1.10A** investigate how the external characterist of an animal are related to where it lives, how it moves, and what it eats

Name _____

Essential Question

How Can We Group Animals?

Set a Purpose

Tell what you want to find out.

_____

_____

Think About the Procedure

1 How do you know which animals belong in the same group?

_____

_____

2 How will you record the groups you make?

_____

© Houghton Mifflin Harcourt Publishing Company

Record Your Data

Color a box to show each way the animal moves.

How Does It Move?

	Walk	**Swim**	**Fly**
duck			
butterfly			
mouse			
fish			
bat			
penguin			
parrot			
alligator			
cow			

Draw Conclusions

How could you tell how an animal moves?

_____

Ask More Questions

What other questions can you ask about classifying animals?

_____

© Houghton Mifflin Harcourt Publishing Company

Picture Cards

Cut out each picture on the dashed lines.

duck

butterfly

mouse

fish

bat

penguin

parrot

alligator

cow

© Houghton Mifflin Harcourt Publishing Company (cr) ©david sanger photography/Alamy; (bl) ©Amazon-Images/Alamy; (tl) ©Juniors Bildarchiv/Alamy; (tc) ©Llawren Lu/Cutcaster; (cl) ©blickwinkel/Alamy; (c) ©WILDLIFE GmbH/Alamy; (bc) ©David Ponton/Design Pics/Corbis; (br) ©Peter Cavanagh/Alamy; (tr) ©blickwinkel/Alamy

TEKS **1.3A** identify and explain a problem such as finding a home for a classroom pet and propose a solution in his/her own words

On the Farm

Farm System

A farm is a kind of system. A system is a group of parts that work together. All parts must work for the whole system to run well. Some parts of a farm are the crops, animals, people, and tools.

Farmers use tools, such as fences, to protect their crops and animals.

© Houghton Mifflin Harcourt Publishing Company (b) ©AgStockImages/Corbis (inset) ©Gerhard Eager/Corbis

What to Do?

Read the story. Then write how you would solve the problem.

You have a small farm. Everything is working well. One day, wind knocks down part of a fence on your farm.

1. How could the broken fence affect the farm?
2. What would you do to fix the problem?

1. _____

_____

_____

2. _____

_____

Build On It!

Design solutions to other problems on a farm. Complete **Design It: Guard the Lettuce!** on the Inquiry Flipchart.

© Houghton Mifflin Harcourt Publishing Company (t) ©Sara Gray/Getty Images

TEKS **1.10C** compare ways that young animals resemble their parents **1.10D** observe and record life cycles of animals such as a chicken, frog, or fish

Lesson **3**

Essential Question

What Are Some Animal Life Cycles?

Engage Your Brain!

Find the answer to the riddle in this lesson.

When is a frog not like a frog?

When it is

a _____.

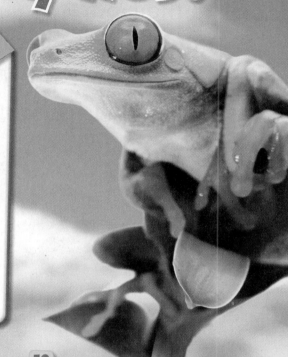

Active Reading

Lesson Vocabulary

① Preview the lesson.

② Write the 5 vocabulary terms here.

_____ _____

_____ _____

_____

Inquiry Flipchart p. 47—Where's the Caterpillar?/What's My Life Cycle?

359

© Houghton Mifflin Harcourt Publishing Company ©Christian Baitg/Photographer's Choice/Getty Images

Animal Start-Ups

A dog can have puppies. A cat can have kittens. Adult animals can **reproduce**, or have young. Animals such as puppies and kittens look like their parents.

Other young animals look very different from their parents. They go through changes to become like their parents.

A young cat looks like its parents.

A young butterfly does not look like its parents.

▶ **Compare how a cat and a kitten are alike.**

_____

© Houghton Mifflin Harcourt Publishing Company   (t) ©Jo Sax/Stone/Getty Images; (c) ©Photodisc/Getty Images ©(bl) ©Scott Bell/Alamy

What's in the Egg?

Many animals begin life by hatching from an egg. Animals change as they grow. The changes that happen to an animal during its life make up its **life cycle**.

▶ Observe the life cycles in the chart. Record the three stages of the life cycles.

_____

_____

Animal Life Cycles

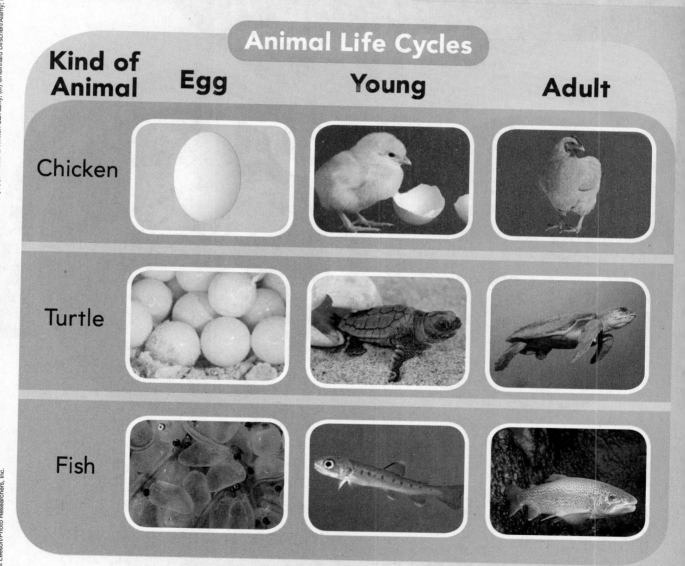

Kind of Animal	Egg	Young	Adult
Chicken			
Turtle			
Fish			

© Houghton Mifflin Harcourt Publishing Company   (tc) ©Getty Images/PhotoDisc; (tr) ©Getty Images/PhotoDisc; (cl) ©Peter Arnold, Inc./Alamy; (c) ©Visual & Written SL/Alamy; (cr) ©Reinhard Dirscherl/Alamy; (bl) ©Theodore Clutter/Photo Researchers, Inc.; (bc) ©Theodore Clutter/Photo Researchers, Inc.; (br)
©Thomas & Pat Leeson/Photo Researchers, Inc.

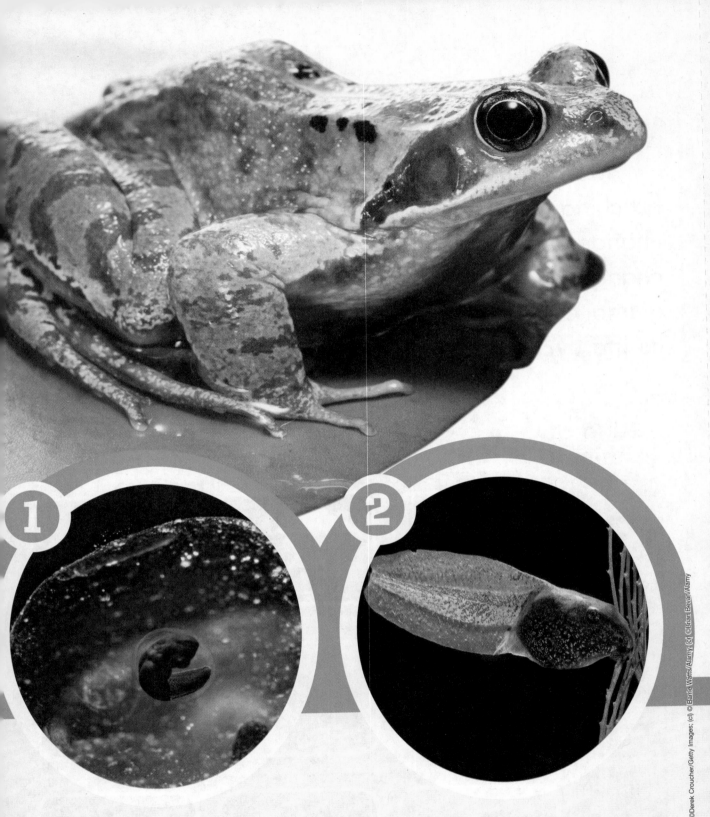

Egg
A frog begins life inside a tiny egg.

Young Tadpole
A **tadpole**, or young frog, hatches. It lives in water. It takes in oxygen with gills.

© Houghton Mifflin Harcourt Publishing Company (t) ©Derek Croucher/Getty Images; (cl) © Barrie Watts/Alamy; (cr) ©Brian Bevan/Alamy

Hatch, Swim, Hop

Did you know that a frog begins life inside a tiny egg? The young frog goes through many changes to become an adult. Observe the frog's life cycle below.

Active Reading

Find the sentence that tells the meaning of **tadpole**. Draw a line under the sentence.

Growing Tadpole

The tadpole gets bigger. It grows four legs. Later, it loses its tail.

Frog

The adult can live on land or in the water. It hops. It breathes with lungs.

© Houghton Mifflin Harcourt Publishing Company (cl) ©Brian Bevan/Alamy; (cr) Derek Croucher/Alamy

363

Polar Parenting

It is late October. A female polar bear gets a shelter ready for her cubs. She digs a den in the snow. The den will keep her young warm and safe. She gives birth in winter.

▶ **Compare how a young polar bear looks like its mother.**

_____

1

2

Newborn
A polar bear cub is born inside the den. It looks a lot like its parents.

Growing Cub
The cub begins to explore outside the den.

© Houghton Mifflin Harcourt Publishing Company (bkgd) ©Steve Bloom Images/Alamy; (cl) ©Jenny E. Ross/Corbis; (cr) ©All Canada Photos/Alamy

We'll stay with our mother for almost three years.

③

④

Young Polar Bear

The young polar bear learns to swim and hunt.

Adult Polar Bear

The adult polar bear can live on its own. It can have its own young

© Houghton Mifflin Harcourt Publishing Company (bl) ©Steve Bloom/Alamy; (cr) All Canada Photos/Alamy

The Mighty Monarch

A butterfly has a life cycle, too. An adult female butterfly lays a tiny egg. The egg is so small it is hard to see. This picture shows a close-up of an egg.

1 egg

▶ Observe the life cycle of a butterfly. Record the four stages it goes through as it grows and changes.

_____

_____

© Houghton Mifflin Harcourt Publishing Company (bkgd) ©George D. Lepp/Photo Researchers, Inc.

2 larva

A tiny **larva**, or caterpillar, hatches from the egg. A caterpillar is a young butterfly. The larva eats a lot. It grows quickly.

Then the larva stops eating and moving. The larva becomes a pupa. It makes a hard covering.

A **pupa** goes through many changes inside the covering. It grows wings.

3 pupa

4 adult

Finally, an adult butterfly comes out of the covering. It can have its own young.

Active Reading

Clue words can help you find the order of events. Draw a box around the clue words **then** and **finally**.

© Houghton Mifflin Harcourt Publishing Company (t) ©Daniel Dempster Photography/Alamy; (c) ©Daniel Dempster Photography/Alamy; (b) Don Farrall/Photographer's Choice RF/Getty Images

Sum It Up!

① Mark It!

Draw an X on the animal that does not look like its young.

② Draw It!

Draw a picture of this animal's mother.

③ Solve It!

Answer the riddle.

I am little now. I will change and grow. Someday I will be an adult cat.

What am I? _____

④ Think About It!

Is a  most like

a  , a , or

a ? Why?

© Houghton Mifflin Harcourt Publishing Company (tl) ©Scott Bell/Alamy; (tc) ©Getty Images/PhotoDisc/PhotoDisc; (cl) ©Getty Images/PhotoDisc; (c) ©Thomas & Pat Leeson/Photo Researchers, Inc.

Name _____

Word Play

Use these words to complete the puzzle.

| tadpole | pupa | larva | reproduce | cycle |

Across

❶ The stage in a butterfly's life cycle after the egg

❷ To make more living things of the same kind

Down

❸ The stage in a butterfly's life between larva and adult

❹ A young frog that lives in water

❺ All the stages of an animal's life make up its life _____.

© Houghton Mifflin Harcourt Publishing Company

Apply Concepts

Compare the life cycle of a butterfly to the life cycle of a polar bear. Record how they are different.

Life Cycles

Butterfly	Polar Bear
A butterfly hatches from an egg.	_____ _____
_____ _____	A polar bear cub drinks milk from its mother's body.
_____ _____	A polar bear cub looks a lot like its parents.
A butterfly larva does not stay with its parents.	_____ _____

Take It Home!

Family Members: Discuss life cycles with your child. Observe and record the life cycle of a chicken, frog, or fish.

© Houghton Mifflin Harcourt Publishing Company

Ask a Zoo Keeper

Now It's Your Turn!

▶ **Describe what a zoo keeper does.**

_____

_____

What does a zoo keeper do?

I feed the animals. I give them water. I make sure that the animals are healthy. I also keep their environments clean.

How do you know when an animal is sick?

Animals can not tell me when they do not feel well. So I observe them carefully. Sometimes an animal eats or moves very little. That could be a sign that the animal is sick.

What else does a zoo keeper do?

I talk to people about the zoo animals. I have fun talking to children. They like animals so much!

© Houghton Mifflin Harcourt Publishing Company ©Christopher Furlong/Staff/Getty Images

Now You Be a Zoo Keeper!

▶ **A tiger cub was born at your zoo. Make a plan to take care of the cub.**

My Zoo Keeper Plan

1 I will _____

_____.

2 I will _____

_____.

3 I will _____

_____.

© Houghton Mifflin Harcourt Publishing Company (br) ©Martin Harvey/Digital Vision/Getty Images; (bkgd) ©Thomas & Pat Leeson/Photo Researchers, Inc.

Vocabulary Review

Use the terms in the box to complete the sentences.

| adaptation |
| larva |
| life cycle |

TEKS 1.10D

1. The changes that happen to an animal during its life make up its

   _____.

TEKS 1.10A

2. Gills are an _____ that let fish take in air from the water.

TEKS 1.10D

3. A butterfly spends its _____ stage as a caterpillar.

Science Concepts

Fill in the letter of the choice that best answers the question.

TEKS 1.10D

4. How is a frog's life cycle the same as a turtle's life cycle?

   Ⓐ Both animals hatch from an egg.

   Ⓑ Both animals have shells.

   Ⓒ Both animals look like their parents when they are born.

TEKS 1.10D

5. You see a butterfly flying. What part of its life cycle is the butterfly in?

   Ⓐ adult

   Ⓑ egg

   Ⓒ larva

© Houghton Mifflin Harcourt Publishing Company

6. What can you tell by looking at the lion's teeth?

Ⓐ It eats meat.
Ⓑ It eats grass.
Ⓒ It eats seeds.

7. Which body part does a rabbit use to move?
Ⓐ flat teeth
Ⓑ strong legs
Ⓒ warm fur

8. How is the zebra using its stripes?

Ⓐ to run
Ⓑ to hide
Ⓒ to stay warm

9. Which animal looks like its parents when it is born?
Ⓐ a butterfly
Ⓑ a frog
Ⓒ a polar bear

© Houghton Mifflin Harcourt Publishing Company

10. Why do seals need a thick layer of body fat?

Ⓐ to keep warm
Ⓑ to move
Ⓒ to hide

11. How are a young duck and a mother duck the same? Compare them.
Ⓐ They both have hair and use legs to walk.
Ⓑ They both have feathers and use wings to fly.
Ⓒ They both have scales and use fins to swim.

12. Which of these animals hatches from an egg?
Ⓐ
Ⓑ
Ⓒ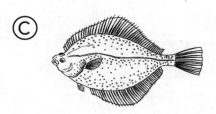

© Houghton Mifflin Harcourt Publishing Company

Inquiry and the Big Idea

Write the answers to these questions.

TEKS 1.10A

13. Look at the animal eating.

    a. What kind of teeth do you think the animal has?

_____

    b. Why do you think so?

_____

_____

TEKS 1.2D, 1.10C, 1.10D

14. Observe the animals.
    Think about their
    life cycles.

    a. Record one way their life cycles are alike.

_____

_____

    b. Record one way their life cycles are different.

_____

_____

© Houghton Mifflin Harcourt Publishing Company

UNIT 10
Plants

© Houghton Mifflin Harcourt Publishing Company (c) ©Gary Holscher/AgStock Images/Corbis; (inset) ©Peter Arnold, Inc./Alamy; (border) ©Nordic/Age Fotostock

Big Idea

Plants have parts that help them grow and change. There are many kinds of plants.

TEKS 1.2A, 1.2B, 1.2D, 1.3A, 1.3C, 1.4A, 1.4B, 1.10B

grapes growing on a vine

I Wonder Why
A plant's leaves need water, light, and air. Why?
Turn the page to find out.

Here's Why The leaves use the water, light, and air to make food.

In this unit, you will explore this Big Idea, the Essential Questions, and the Investigations on the Inquiry Flipchart.

Levels of Inquiry Key ■ DIRECTED ■ GUIDED ■ INDEPENDENT

Big Idea Plants have parts that help them grow and change. There are many kinds of plants.

Essential Questions

Lesson 1 What Are Some Parts of Plants? 379
Inquiry Flipchart p. 48—Are All Seeds Alike?/What Parts Do You See?

People in Science: Dr. Norma Alcantar 389

Lesson 2 How Are Plants Different? 391
Inquiry Flipchart p. 49—Rubbed Leaf Collection/Fantastic Flowers

Inquiry Lesson 3 How Can We Compare Leaves? . . . 401
Inquiry Flipchart p. 50—How Can We Compare Leaves?

S.T.E.M. Engineering and Technology: Warm It Up 403
Inquiry Flipchart p. 51—Design It: Greenhouse

Unit 10 Review 405

Now I Get the Big Idea!

Science Notebook

Before you begin each lesson, be sure to write your thoughts about the Essential Question.

Essential Question

What Are Some Parts of Plants?

🧠 Engage Your Brain!

Find the answer to the question in the lesson.

What holds this tree in place?

its _____

Active Reading

Lesson Vocabulary

1 Preview the lesson.

2 Write the 6 vocabulary terms here.

_____   _____

_____   _____

_____   _____

Inquiry Flipchart p. 48—Are All Seeds Alike?/What Parts Do You See?

379

© Houghton Mifflin Harcourt Publishing Company ©Paul Plebina/Getty Images

A Plant's Makeup

A plant has parts that help it grow and change.

Taking Root

A plant has roots that grow into the soil. The **roots** hold the plant in place. They take in water from the soil. They take in other things from the soil that the plant needs.

Active Reading

A detail is a fact about a main idea. Draw one line under a detail. Draw an arrow to the main idea it tells about.

roots

© Houghton Mifflin Harcourt Publishing Company (b) ©Theo Allofs/Getty Images

Stems Stand Tall

The **stem** holds up the plant. It takes water from the roots to the other parts of the plant.

A flower has a thin, soft stem. A tree has a thick, woody stem.

stems

▶ Identify the roots and stems on these pages. Circle the roots. Put a box around the stems. Then compare how they are alike and different.

_____

_____

© Houghton Mifflin Harcourt Publishing Company   (tr) ©Radius Images/Corbis; (bl) ©Kei Uesugi/Getty Images

Leaves at Work

A **leaf** is a plant part that makes food for the plant. It uses light, air, and water.

Active Reading

Find the sentence that tells the meaning of **leaf**. Draw a line under the sentence.

Leaves can be different shapes and sizes.

banana leaf

pine needles

clover

ash

red maple

© Houghton Mifflin Harcourt Publishing Company   (l) © Joson/Corbis; (bc) ©Datacraft/Getty Images; (c) ©D. Hurst/Alamy; (br) ©WILDLIFE GmbH/Alamy

Flowers, Seeds, and Fruit

Many plants have flowers. A **flower** is a plant part that makes seeds. A new plant may grow from a **seed**. The new plant will look like the plant that made the seed.

Many flowers grow into fruits. A **fruit** holds seeds.

fruit

flower

seed

▶ **Identify parts of plants. Draw a circle around the leaves. Draw an X on the flowers, fruits, and seeds. Then compare how they are alike and different.**

_____

_____

© Houghton Mifflin Harcourt Publishing Company (cr) ©Creativ Studio Heinemann/Westend61/Corbis

Plant Power

We use plants for food. We also use plants to make things. Mint leaves are used in some toothpastes. Flowers make perfume smell good. Woody stems help make our homes. We even use plants to make some medicines. What other plant uses can you name?

© Houghton Mifflin Harcourt Publishing Company   (bkgd) ©Jane MacDonald/Alamy

Do the Math!
Solve a Problem

Look at the tomatoes. Use them to help you solve this problem.

A farmer has 24 tomatoes.
He picks 11 tomatoes.
How many are left?

_____ - _____ = _____

© Houghton Mifflin Harcourt Publishing Company   (bkgd) ©Ilene MacDonald/Alamy

Sum It Up!

① Choose It!

Identify the plant part that takes in water. Circle it.

② Solve It!

Solve each riddle.

I can be thick or thin.
I can be short or tall.
I help a plant get water and hold it up so it won't fall.

What am I?

_____

I can be different colors, shapes, and sizes.
I may fall to the ground.
I take in light and air to make food for a plant since it can't move around.

What am I?

_____

386

© Houghton Mifflin Harcourt Publishing Company© Houghton Mifflin Harcourt Publishing Company

Name _____

Word Play

Identify the parts of the plant. Label it using words from the box.

flower	leaf	roots	stem

_____

_____

_____

_____

© Houghton Mifflin Harcourt Publishing Company

Apply Concepts

Identify which plant parts a plant needs.

Problem	Solution
❶ I need a plant part to hold seeds. What part do I need?	_____
❷ I need a plant part to take in water. What part do I need?	_____
❸ I need a plant part to make fruit. What part do I need?	_____
❹ I need a plant part to make food. What part do I need?	_____
❺ I need a plant part to hold me up. What part do I need?	_____
❻ I need a plant part to make a plant just like me. What part do I need?	_____

Take It Home!

Family Members: Encourage your child to identify and compare the parts of a plant. Help your child name plants you eat and use everyday.

© Houghton Mifflin Harcourt Publishing Company

Get to Know...
Dr. Norma Alcantar

Dr. Norma Alcantar studies materials. She makes them more useful. Dr. Alcantar wanted to find a way to make water clean.

She learned that some people in Mexico used prickly pear cactus plants to clean water. The plants have a gooey material. Dr. Alcantar studied it. She used the goo to make water clean.

Fun Fact

She learned about using this kind of cactus from her grandmother.

© Houghton Mifflin Harcourt Publishing Company (bkgd) ©Steve Taylor/Getty Images; (cr) ©Derek Hall/Dorling Kindersley/Getty Images

Clean It!

▶ Answer the questions about Dr. Alcantar's work.

1 Describe what Dr. Alcantar does.

_____

_____

_____

2 Where did Dr. Alcantar get the idea for using the prickly pear cactus in her studies?

_____

_____

3 Why is Dr. Alcantar's work important?

_____

_____

_____

4 What does Dr. Alcantar use from the cactus to make clean water?

_____

© Houghton Mifflin Harcourt Publishing Company

Essential Question

How Are Plants Different?

Engage Your Brain!

Find the answer to the question in the lesson.

How is this plant like some animals?

_____

_____ .

Active Reading

Lesson Vocabulary

1 Preview the lesson.

2 Write the 2 vocabulary terms here.

_____   _____

Is It a Plant?

Plants are living things, like animals. Plants are also different from animals.

Plants can not move like animals. They stay in one place. Green plants use light, water, and air to make their own food. Animals eat plants or other animals.

Active Reading

When you compare things, you find out ways they are alike. Draw triangles around two things that are being compared.

Houghton Mifflin Harcourt Publishing Company (bkgd) ©Renee Lynn/Corbis

Plants and Animals

▶ **Complete the chart to tell how plants and animals are different.**

	Plants	Animals
make their own food		
eat plants or animals		
move around on their own		
grow and change		

A Venus flytrap is a strange plant. It moves its leaves to catch insects and spiders. Then it eats what it catches.

© Houghton Mifflin Harcourt Publishing Company (b) ©Kim Taylor and Jane Burton/Getty Images

Plenty of Plants

How can you tell plants apart? You can compare their parts. They have different leaves. They have different shapes. They can be big or small.

Some plants have soft, thin stems. Some have thick, woody stems.

Trees
- tall
- woody trunk
- many branches
- different leaves
- long life

oak tree

© Houghton Mifflin Harcourt Publishing Company (Nakad) (Image Source/Corbis

Shrubs

- shorter than trees
- smaller, woody stems
- smaller branches
- different leaves
- long life

boxwood shrub

Grasses

- small plants
- soft stems
- long, thin leaves
- shorter life

ornamental grasses

► **Compare parts of plants. Circle the names of the plants with woody stems. Draw a line under the name of the plant with soft stems.**

© Houghton Mifflin Harcourt Publishing Company (bkgd) ©Image Source/Alamy; (tr) ©RF Company/Alamy; (br) ©Cubo Images Srl/Alamy

Plants with Flowers

Some plants have flowers. **Flowers** make a plant's seeds. Flowers can grow on small plants. They can also grow on shrubs and trees. Where have you seen flowers?

hibiscus plant

▶ **Identify the plant part that makes seeds.**

_____

© Houghton Mifflin Harcourt Publishing Company   (br) ©Michael Wong/Getty Images

Plants with Cones

Some plants have cones. **Cones** hold a plant's seeds. Cones grow on some trees. Where have you seen cones?

Active Reading

A detail is a fact about a main idea. Draw one line under a detail. Draw an arrow to the main idea it tells about.

pinecone

pine tree

© Houghton Mifflin Harcourt Publishing Company (bl) ©Zefiryn Pagowski/Alamy; (br) ©imagebroker/Alamy

Sum It Up!

① Circle It!

Circle the plant that has cones.

② Choose It!

Circle each group of words that tells about an animal.

eats plants or animals

makes its own food

grows and changes

moves around on its own

③ Solve It!

Solve the riddle.

Some living things fly.
Some walk, run, or swim.
I do not move on my own.
I stay in one place.

What am I? _____

© Houghton Mifflin Harcourt Publishing Company

Name _____

Word Play

Color the letters to spell the vocabulary words.
Write the words to complete the sentences.

c	t	o	t	r	e	e
f	l	o	w	e	r	o
t	a	g	l	d	e	i
e	j	c	o	n	e	b
i	r	s	w	g	h	l
k	e	m	e	o	a	d
r	s	h	r	u	b	Y

> flower   shrub
> cone   tree

① A tall plant with a woody stem
is a _____ .

② A tree without a flower may have
a _____ .

③ A _____ makes seeds.

④ A plant that is smaller than a tree
is a _____ .

© Houghton Mifflin Harcourt Publishing Company

Complete the diagram to tell how plants and animals are alike and different.

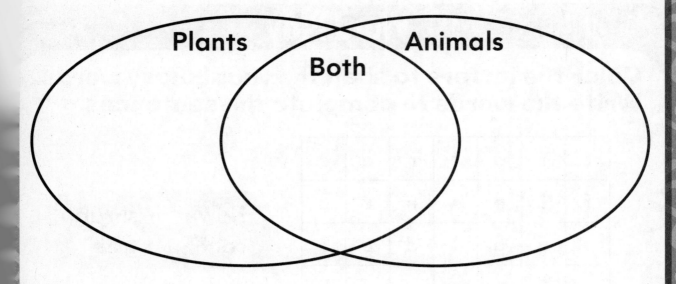

Plants   Both   Animals

❶ Compare plant stems. How are they different?

_____

_____

❷ Write 1, 2, and 3 to put the plants in size order.

Start with the smallest plant.

____ tree   ____ grass   ____ shrub

Take It Home!

Family Members: Take a neighborhood walk with your child. Ask your child to compare plants and the different parts they have.

© Houghton Mifflin Harcourt Publishing Company

Inquiry Flipchart p. 50

TEKS **1.2A** ask questions about organisms, objects, and events observed the natural world **1.2B** plan and condu simple descriptive investigations such as ways objects move **1.2D** record and organize data using pictures, numbers, and words **1.4A** collect and compare information using tools, including . . . non-standard measuring items such as paper clips and clothespins . . . **1.4B** measure and compare organisms and objects using non-standard units **1.10B** identify and compare parts of plants

Name _____

Essential Question

How Can We Compare Leaves?

Set a Purpose

Tell what you want to find out.

_____

_____

Think About the Procedure

1 Why do you measure each leaf?

_____

2 How will you compare the leaves by size?

_____

_____

© Houghton Mifflin Harcourt Publishing Company

Record Your Data

Record the length of each leaf. Circle the shortest leaf in each row. Draw an X on the longest leaf in each row.

Leaf Chart

Leaf 1	Leaf 2	Leaf 3
about _____ paper clips long	about _____ paper clips long	about _____ paper clips long
about _____ clothespins long	about _____ clothespins long	about _____ clothespins long

Draw Conclusions

Compare the measurements. Were they different? Why?

_____

_____

Ask More Questions

What other questions could you ask about comparing leaves?

_____

© Houghton Mifflin Harcourt Publishing Company

TEKS 1.3A identify and explain a problem such as finding a home for a classroom pet and propose a solution in his/her own words

Warm It Up

Compare Greenhouses

Greenhouses are made of glass or plastic. Glass and plastic let in light. They also keep in heat. Light and heat help plants grow. Different plants can be grown at the same time.

indoor greenhouse

outdoor greenhouse

- needs only a small space
- for small plants only
- stays warm in winter

- needs a large space
- for small or large plants
- needs heating in winter

© Houghton Mifflin Harcourt Publishing Company (cr) ©SGM SGM/photolibrary

S.T.E.M.
continued

Which Greenhouse?

Read the problem below.
Then answer the questions.

You want to grow a large plant.
You have a lot of outdoor space.
The weather is not very cold.
Which greenhouse would you
choose? Why?

_____

_____

_____

_____

Build On It!

Design your own indoor greenhouse. Complete
Design It: Greenhouse on the Inquiry Flipchart.

© Houghton Mifflin Harcourt Publishing Company   (t) ©Tim Hill/Alamy

Name _____

Vocabulary Review

Use the terms in the box to complete the sentences.

> leaf
> roots
> seed

TEKS 1.10B

1. A new plant may grow from a

   _____.

TEKS 1.10B

2. A plant is held in place by its

   _____.

TEKS 1.10B

3. The plant part that makes food
   is the _____.

Science Concepts

Fill in the letter of the choice that best answers the question.

TEKS 1.10B

4. Trey compares an apple and a pinecone. How are they alike?

   Ⓐ They both are fruits.
   Ⓑ They both hold seeds.
   Ⓒ They both grow on the same kind of tree.

TEKS 1.2B, 1.10B

5. Umi is planning an investigation. She wants to plant something that will live a long time, but will not grow very tall. Which of these should she plant?

   Ⓐ grass
   Ⓑ shrub
   Ⓒ tree

© Houghton Mifflin Harcourt Publishing Company

5. Pavil sorted leaves. This picture shows one group.

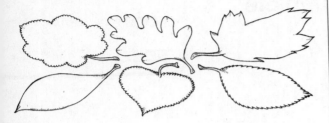

Which choice **best** describes how she sorted the leaves?

Ⓐ by size

Ⓑ by shape

Ⓒ by number of points

7. Which of these plant parts can be identified as a stem?

Ⓐ apple

Ⓑ tree trunk

Ⓒ pine needle

8. Which of these is a way that all plants are alike?

Ⓐ They have flowers.

Ⓑ They grow tall and have thick stems.

Ⓒ They make their own food.

9. Which plant part does number 3 show?

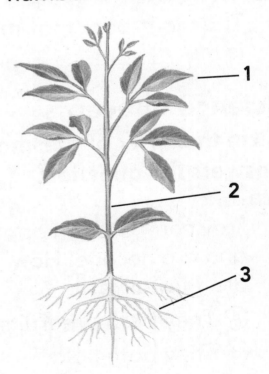

Ⓐ leaf

Ⓑ stem

Ⓒ roots

© Houghton Mifflin Harcourt Publishing Company

10. Alex is comparing trees, shrubs, and grasses. He records his observations. Which sentence tells how all three are the same?

Ⓐ They grow and change.

Ⓑ They cannot make their own food.

Ⓒ They can move on their own.

11. Sara is identifying plant parts. What kind of stems do shrubs have?

Ⓐ green stems

Ⓑ soft stems

Ⓒ woody stems

12. Read these steps for how a plant gets and uses water.

1. The roots take in water from the soil.

2. _____?_____

3. The leaves use water to make food.

Which step is missing?

Ⓐ The plant grows taller.

Ⓑ The flowers grow into fruit.

Ⓒ Water moves through the stem to all of the leaves.

© Houghton Mifflin Harcourt Publishing Company

Inquiry and the Big Idea
Write the answers to these questions.

TEKS 1.10B

13. Explain what each of these plant parts does.

a. flowers

_____

b. fruits

_____

c. seeds

_____

TEKS 1.10B

14. Look at the pictures. Compare the stems of the tree and the grass.

a. How are they different?

_____

_____

b. How are they the same?

_____

© Houghton Mifflin Harcourt Publishing Company

Interactive Glossary

This Interactive Glossary will help you learn how to spell a vocabulary term. The Glossary will give you the meaning of the term. It will also show you a picture to help you understand what the term means.

Where you see **Your Turn** write your own words or draw your own picture to help you remember what the term means.

A

adaptation A body part or behavior that helps a living thing survive. (p. 342)

Your Turn

attract To pull toward something. (p. 138)

C

clay Small bits of rock. It holds water so well that clay sticks together. (p. 193)

© Houghton Mifflin Harcourt Publishing Company

Interactive Glossary

condense To change from a gas to a liquid. (p. 111)

conservation A way to protect resources and materials. (p. 220)

cone The part of a nonflowering plant that holds the plant's seeds. (p. 397)

design process A plan with steps that help engineers find good solutions. (p. 55)

Your Turn

© Houghton Mifflin Harcourt Publishing Company   (bl) ©Zefryn Pagowski/Alamy

E

electricity A form of energy. People produce electricity by using energy from other sources. (p. 128)

engineer Someone who uses math and science to solve problems. (p. 54)

environment All the living and nonliving things in a place. (pp. 310, 316)

energy Something that causes matter to move or change. Heat and light are kinds of energy. (p. 124)

Your Turn

© Houghton Mifflin Harcourt Publishing Company   (tl) ©Tom Salyer/Alamy Images; (tr) ©Tim Pannell/Corbis; (br) ©Raimund Koch/Corbis; (bl) ©Michele Falzone/Photographer's Choice/Getty Images

Interactive Glossary

evaporate To change from a liquid to a gas. (p. 110)

food chain A path that shows how energy moves from plants to animals. (p. 322)

F

flower The part of a plant that makes seeds. (pp. 383, 396)

Your Turn

© Houghton Mifflin Harcourt Publishing Company (cr) ©Marvin Dembinsky Photo Associates/Alamy; (bl) ©Michael Wong/Getty Images; (br) ©Rick & Nora Bowers/Alamy

force Something that makes an object move or stop moving. (p. 158)

fruit The part of the plant that holds seeds. (p. 383)

freeze To change from a liquid to a solid. (p. 106)

Your Turn

© Houghton Mifflin Harcourt Publishing Company   (bl) ©Richard Prudhomme/Demotix/Corbis

Interactive Glossary

H

heat Energy that makes things warmer. It moves from something warmer to something cooler. (p. 125)

human-made Materials made by people. (p. 72)

Your Turn →

I

inquiry skills Skills that help you find out information. (p. 14)

investigation A test that scientists do. (p. 36)

© Houghton Mifflin Harcourt Publishing Company

L

lake A body of fresh water with land all around it. (p. 205)

leaf The part of a plant that makes food for the plant. A leaf uses light, air, and water to make food. (p. 382)

Your Turn

larva Another name for a caterpillar. (p. 367)

© Houghton Mifflin Harcourt Publishing Company   (tl) ©Theo Allofs/CORBIS; (tr) ©Wildlife GmbH/Alamy

Interactive Glossary

life cycle Changes that happen to an animal or a plant during its life. (p. 361)

light A kind of energy that lets us see. (p. 125)

living things Things that are living. People, animals, and plants are living things because they need food, water, air, and space to live. They grow, change, and reproduce. (p. 306)

M

magnet An object that can pull things made of iron or steel. A magnet can push or pull other magnets. (p. 136)

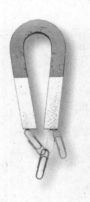

Your Turn

© Houghton Mifflin Harcourt Publishing Company

magnify To make something look bigger. A telescope magnifies the moon. (p. 278)

melt To change from a solid to a liquid. (p. 108)

Your Turn

materials What objects are made of. (p. 70)

matter Anything that takes up space. (p. 90)

moon A large sphere, or ball, of rock. (p. 276)

© Houghton Mifflin Harcourt Publishing Company (br) ©John Lund/Getty Images

motion Movement. When something is in motion, it is moving. (p. 146)

natural Materials found in nature. (p. 72)

natural resource Anything from nature that people can use. (p. 178)

nonliving things Things that are not alive. Nonliving things do not need food, air, and water. They do not grow and change. (p. 308)

Your Turn

© Houghton Mifflin Harcourt Publishing Company   (cl) ©Lance Nelson/Stock Photos/Corbis

O

ocean A large body of salty water. (p. 206)

pollution Waste that harms land, water, and air. (p. 218)

P

phases The shapes of the moon you see as it moves. (p. 289)

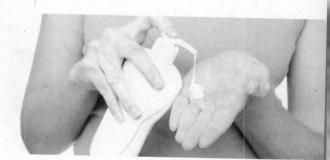

product Something made by people or machines for people to use. (p. 179)

pole A place on a magnet where the pull is the strongest. (p. 137)

Your Turn

© Houghton Mifflin Harcourt Publishing Company   (tl) ©David Pu'u/CORBIS

property One part of what something is like. Color, size, and shape are each a property. (pp. 92, 194)

push To move an object away from you. (p. 158)

Your Turn

pull To move an object closer to you. (p. 158)

R

recycle To use the materials in old things to make new things. (p. 222)

pupa The part of a life cycle when a caterpillar changes into a butterfly. (p. 367)

© Houghton Mifflin Harcourt Publishing Company (tl) ©shinypix/Alamy Images

reduce To use less of a resource. (p. 222)

reproduce To make new living things like oneself. (pp. 306, 360)

repel To push away from something. (p. 140)

Your Turn

reuse To use a resource again. (p. 222)

river A large body of flowing water. (p. 204)

© Houghton Mifflin Harcourt Publishing Company   (br) ©Rolf Richardson/Robert Harding World Imagery/Corbis

rock A hard, nonliving object from the ground. (p. 182)

roots The part of a plant that holds the plant in place. The roots take in water and nutrients. (p. 380)

Your Turn

S

sand Large bits of rock. It does not hold water well. (p. 193)

science tools Tools people use to find out about things. (p. 26)

© Houghton Mifflin Harcourt Publishing Company   (t) ©Bets LaRue/Alamy; (bl) ©Theo Allofs/Getty Images

season A time of year that has a certain kind of weather. The four seasons are spring, summer, fall, and winter. (p. 254)

seed The part of a plant that new plants grow from. (p. 383)

senses The way you observe and learn. The five senses are sight, hearing, smell, taste, and touch. (p. 4)

shadow A dark place made where an object blocks light. (p. 287)

shelter A place where an animal can be safe. (p. 316)

Your Turn

© Houghton Mifflin Harcourt Publishing Company (tl) ©Oxford Picture Library/Alamy

silt Medium bits of rock. It holds water fairly well. (p. 193)

speed The measure of how fast something moves. (p. 146)

soil It is made up of small pieces of rock and once-living things. It is the top layer of Earth. (pp. 183, 190)

star An object in the sky that gives off its own light. The sun is the closest star to Earth. (p. 274)

Your Turn

sound A kind of energy you can hear. (p. 125)

© Houghton Mifflin Harcourt Publishing Company

T

stem The part of a plant that holds up the plant. (p. 381)

tadpole A young frog that comes out of an egg. It has gills to take in oxygen from the water. (p. 362)

stream A small body of flowing water. (p. 204)

sun The star closest to Earth. (p. 274)

telescope A tool that helps magnify things in the sky. (p. 278)

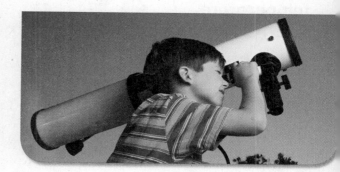

© Houghton Mifflin Harcourt Publishing Company (tl) ©Kei Uesugi/Getty Images; (tr) ©Brian Bevan/Alamy

Interactive Glossary

temperature A measure of how hot or cold something is. (pp. 95, 238)

texture What an object feels like. (p. 92)

thermometer A tool used to measure temperature. (p. 27)

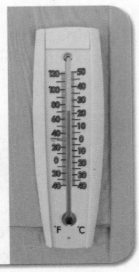

weather What the air outside is like. (p. 236)

Your Turn

© Houghton Mifflin Harcourt Publishing Company   (tr) ©Darby Sawchuk/Alamy

weather pattern A change in the weather that repeats. (p. 254)

weight The measure of how heavy an object feels. (p. 94)

wind Air that moves. (p. 236)

Your Turn

© Houghton Mifflin Harcourt Publishing Company (l) ©Dennis MacDonald/Alamy Images

windsock A tool used to show the direction of the wind. (p. 240)

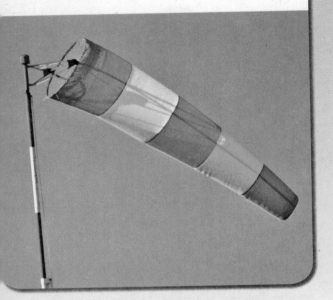

© Houghton Mifflin Harcourt Publishing Company

A

Active Reading. *See*
Reading Skills
adaptations, 342
   animal movement,
     344–345
   animals, 341–349
   for eating, 346–347
   for hiding
     (camouflage),
     348–349
afternoon, 286
air. *See also* **wind**
   as natural resource,
     178
   pollution in, 218–219
Alcantar, Norma,
   389–390
amphibians
   frog, 344, 349,
     362–363
   tadpole, 362–363
   toad, 323
Anderson, Mary, 45–46
animals. *See also*
   amphibians; birds;
   fish and ocean
   animals; insects
   adaptations, 341–349
   Arctic fox, 320
   bison, 321
   cat, 360
   cheetah, 344–345
   chipmunk, 259
   deer, 303–304

   in desert, 319
   desert hare, 319
   differences among,
     341–349
   elephant, 343
   fall season, 258–259
   in food chain, 322–323
   fox, 316
   guinea pig, 325
   hare, 257, 261, 319
   horse, 325, 346
   kitten, 360
   leopard, 318
   life cycles, 359–367
   lion, 346
   monkey, 344
   movement of,
     344–345
   as natural resources,
     180–181
   needs of, 316–325
   in ocean, 317
   pets, 324–325
   plants and, 392–393
   polar bear, 364–365
   prairie dog, 321
   in rain forest, 318
   reproduction, 360–361
   reptiles, 319, 361
   safety needs of,
     333–334
   seasonal changes,
     255–257
   shelter, as basic need,
     316
   spring season,
     254–255

   summer season,
     256–257
   teeth, 346
   tiger, 349
   in tundra, 320
   walrus, 342
   winter season, 260–261
aquarium, 1
architects, 81
Ask More Questions,
   12, 24, 66, 80, 104,
   156, 200, 202, 248,
   296, 332, 354, 402
attract, 138
attraction, magnets,
   138–139
automobile windshield
   wipers, 45–46

B

back and forth motion,
   149, 163
back scratcher,
   designing, 56–61
Bacon-Bercey, June,
   251
balance (tool), 27
beach clean-up,
   175–176
beaks, 346–347
bicycles, 68–69
birds
   beak, 346–347
   cardinal, 347
   chicken eggs, 361
   feathers, 349

© Houghton Mifflin Harcourt Publishing Company

Index

owl, 349
red-tailed hawk, 321
seasonal changes, 255
spoonbill, 339–340
wings, 345
woodpecker, 347
**body fat, to keep
warm, 342–343**
**build, in design
process, 55, 58–59**

Careers in Science
forest ranger, 329–330
polymer scientist,
101–102
zoo keeper, 371–372
**Carver, George
Washington, 187–188**
**car windshield wipers,
45–46**
**cause and effect, 114,
168**
**chocolate chip cookie
recipe, 115**
classify, 16, 73
clay, 193
closer, 162
clouds, 274
cloudy day, 290–291
clue words, 36, 58
cold, 95
color
for hiding
(camouflage),
348–349

of leaves, 382
as property of matter,
93
of soil, 195
communicate
in design process,
55, 61
scientific inquiry, 16
compare, 14
condensation, 111
condense, 111
cones, 397
cooking tools, 115–116
**cooling matter,
106–107, 111**
cotton jeans, 74–75

**dams, for energy
production, 130**
daytime sky, 274–275
desert, 319
**design process,
55–61**
communicate, 55, 61
find a problem,
55, 56–57
plan and build,
55, 58–59
redesign, 55, 61
test and improve,
55, 60
**Details. *See* Main Idea
and Details**

Do the Math!
compare numbers,
242–243
compare solid shapes,
277
make a bar graph,
147
measure length, 31
model fractions, 207
order by weight, 94
solve a problem, 131,
325, 385
solve a word problem,
225, 347
**Draw Conclusions, 12,
18, 24, 39, 66, 80,
104, 156, 200, 202,
248, 296, 332, 354,
402**

Earth
movement of, 286–287
phases of the moon,
288–289
eggs
chicken, 361
fish, 361
frog, 362
life cycles, 361
monarch butterfly, 366
reptiles, 361
turtle, 361

© Houghton Mifflin Harcourt Publishing Company

electricity, 128–129
energy, 124
  all around, 126–127
  electricity at home, 128–129
  kinds of, 130–131
  using, 123–131
Engineering and Technology. *See also* STEM (Science, Technology, Engineering, and Mathematics)
  airplanes, 169–170
  animal habitat, 333–334
  engineers, 51–61
  farms, 357–358
  flashlights, 297–298
  greenhouses, 403–404
  kitchen and cooking, 115–116
  weather tools, 265–266
engineers, 54
  how do engineers work?, 51–61
  as problem solvers, 54–55
environment, 310, 316
  adaptations, 341–349
  desert, 319
  living things in, 310–311, 315–325
  nonliving things in, 308–311, 316

ocean, 206–207, 317
prairie, 321
rain forest, 318
tundra, 320
evaporate, 110
evaporation, 110
everyday materials, 74–75

F

fall season, 258–259
farther, 162
feathers, 349
fins, 345
first, as clue word, 36
fish and ocean animals
  eggs, 361
  fins, 345
  gills, 343
  jellyfish, 317
  seahorse, 1, 2, 348
flashlights, 297–298
flowers, 383, 396
food and eating, 346–347
food chains, 322–323
force, 158
  change location of object, 162–163
  gravity, 165
  motion and, 145–149, 157–165
  push or pull, 157, 158–159

speed, 146, 160–161
  using, 160–163
forest ranger, 329–330
freeze, 106
freezing, 106–107, 233–234
fresh water, 204–205
fruit, 383

G

Galileo Galilei, 283–284
gases, 110, 111
gills, 343, 362
grasses, 395
gravity, 165
greenhouses, 403–404

H

hand lens, 26
hearing, 6
heat, 125
  as energy, 126–127
  heating matter, 108–109, 110
heavy, 94
hiding (camouflage), as adaptation, 348–349
home, electricity at, 128–129
hot, 95
human-made materials, 72–73
hypothesize, 17, 37

© Houghton Mifflin Harcourt Publishing Company

Index

icicles, 233–234
improve, in design process, 55, 60
indoor science safety rules, xxiii
infer, 18
inquiry. *See* **scientific inquiry**
Inquiry Skills, 13–19
 Ask More Questions, 12, 24, 66, 80, 104, 156, 200, 202, 248, 296, 332, 354, 402
 Draw Conclusions, 12, 18, 24, 39, 66, 80, 104, 156, 200, 202, 248, 296, 332, 354, 402
 Record Your Data, 12, 24, 40–41, 66, 80, 104, 156, 200, 202, 248, 296, 332, 354, 402
 Set a Purpose, 11, 23, 65, 79, 103, 155, 199, 201, 247, 295, 331, 353, 401
 Think About the Procedure, 11, 23, 65, 79, 103, 155, 199, 201, 247, 295, 331, 353, 401
inquiry skills, 14

insects
 caterpillar, 367
 cricket, 323
 monarch butterfly, 360, 366–367
 walking stick, 341
investigations, 36

jeans, 74–75

Kearns, Robert, 46

lakes, 205
land, pollution of, 218–219
larva, 367
leaf (leaves), 382
length, measuring, 31
life cycles, 359–367. *See also* **eggs; reproduction**
 of amphibians, 362–363
 of animals, 359–367
 of insects, 360, 366–367
light, 125
light (energy), 125, 126–127
light (weight), 94

liquids
 condensation, 111
 evaporation, 110
 freezing, 106–107, 233–234
 melting, 108–109
living things, 306. *See also* **animals; plants**
lungs, 363

magnets, 136
 attracts or repels, 138–141
 moving objects with, 135–141
 poles of, 137, 139, 141
 repulsion, 140–141
magnify, 278
Main Idea and Details, 4, 38, 40, 68, 90, 136, 140, 162, 178, 206, 208, 236, 258, 274, 276, 286, 288, 346, 397
materials, 70. *See also* **natural resources**
 everyday, 74–75
 human-made, 72–73
 natural, 72–73, 389
 objects, 67–75
matter, 90. *See also* **liquids; objects**
 changes in, 105–111
 cooling, 106–107, 111

© Houghton Mifflin Harcourt Publishing Company

gases, 110, 111
heating, 108–109, 110
properties of, 89–97
solids, 106–109
states of, 105–111
measurement
of length, 31
scientific inquiry, 15
of temperature, 27, 103–104
tools for, 27, 28–30
units for, 29
of weather, 238–243, 265–266
of wind, 241
measuring cup, 27
melt, 108
melting, 108–109
miniature golf course, 121–122
modeling, 19
moon (of Earth), 276
as object in the sky, 271–272
phases of, 288–289
morning, 286
motion, 146
force and, 145–149, 157–165
kinds of, 148–149
of objects, 145–149
speed, 146, 160–161
movement
of animals, 344–345
phases of the moon, 288–289

natural materials, 72–73, 389
natural resources, 175–183
air, 178
plants and animals, 180–181
pollution, 217–221
reduce, reuse, recycle, 222–225
rocks, 182
saving, 217–225
soil, 183
water, 179
nearer, 162
Newton, Isaac, 153–154
nighttime sky, 276–279
nonliving things, 308–311, 316
noon, 286–287

objects, 67–75. *See also* **materials**
changing the movement of, 157–165
composition of, 72–75
location changed by force, 162–163
movement of, 135–141, 145–149, 157–165
moving with magnets, 135–141

parts of, 68–71
properties of, 89–97
observe
properties of objects, 89–97
scientific inquiry, 14, 36, 40
oceans, 206, 206–207, 317. *See also* **fish and ocean animals**
once-living things in soil, 190–193, 195
orbit, phases of the moon, 288–289
order. *See* **sequence**
outdoor science safety rules, xxiv

peanuts, 187–188
People in Science
Alcantar, Norma, 389–390
Anderson, Mary, 45–46
Bacon-Bercey, June, 251
Carver, George Washington, 187–188
Galileo Galilei, 283–284
Newton, Isaac, 153–154
Tsui, Eugene, 81–82

© Houghton Mifflin Harcourt Publishing Company

Index

phases, 289
  of the moon, 288–289
plan
  an investigation, 17, 37
  in design process, 55,
    58–59
plants, 391–397. *See*
  also **trees**
  animals and, 392–393
  Arctic flowers, 320
  ash tree, 382
  banana leaf, 382
  boxwood shrub, 395
  clover, 382
  coneflowers, 321
  dandelion, 381
  in desert, 319
  fall season, 258–259
  flowers, 383
  in food chain, 322
  fruit, 383
  grape vine, 377–378
  grass, 322, 395
  hibiscus flower, 396
  Joshua tree, 319
  kelp, 317
  kinds of, 394–397
  leaf (leaves), 382
  marigold, 380
  as natural resources,
    180–181
  in ocean, 317
  ornamental grasses,
    395
  parts of, 380–383
  pine needles, 382
  in prairie, 321

  red maple, 382
  roots, 380
  seasonal changes,
    254–261
  seeds, 383
  shrubs, 395
  spring season, 254–255
  stems, 381
  summer season,
    256–257
  tree, 381
  uses of, 384–385
  Venus flytrap, 391, 393
  winter season,
    260–261
playground, 51–52
poles, magnetic, 137,
  139–141
pollution, 218
  in land, water, and air,
    218–219
  reduce, reuse, recycle,
    222–225
  solutions to, 220–221
polymer scientist,
  101–102
prairie, 321
predict, 15
predict the weather,
  242–243
problem
  in design process, 55,
    56–57
  solve a problem in
    math, 225, 325
problem solvers,
  engineers as, 54–55

product, 179
properties of matter,
  89–97
property, 92, 194
pull, 157, 158, 159
pupa, 367
push, 157, 158–159

R

rain forest, 318
rain gauge, 239
Reading Skills, 3, 4, 13,
  14, 25, 26, 28, 35, 36,
  38, 40, 53, 54, 58, 67,
  68, 70, 74, 89, 90,
  92, 105, 106, 111, 123,
  124, 128, 135, 136,
  140, 145, 149, 157,
  159, 162, 177, 178,
  182, 189, 190, 192,
  194, 203, 206, 208,
  217, 218, 222, 235,
  236, 238, 253, 254,
  258, 273–274, 276,
  285, 286, 305, 308,
  310, 315, 316, 321,
  341, 342, 346, 359,
  363, 367, 379, 380,
  382, 391, 392, 397
Record Data, 12, 24,
  40–41, 66, 80, 104,
  156, 200, 202, 248,
  296, 332, 354, 402
recycle, 222–225
redesign, in design
  process, 55, 61

© Houghton Mifflin Harcourt Publishing Company

reduce, 222–223
repel, 140
reproduce, 306, 360
reproduction, 306, 311
  of animals, 360–361
reptiles
  Gila monster, 319
  turtle eggs, 361
repulsion, magnets,
  140–141
resources. See natural
  resources
reuse, 222–225
rivers, 204
rock, 182
  as natural resource,
    182
  in soil, 190–191, 193,
    195
roller coaster, 164–165
roots, 380
round and round
  motion, 149
ruler, 27

S

safety
  in science, xxiii–xxiv
  water, 210–211
salt water (ocean),
  206–207, 317
sand, 193
sandcastle, 87–88
science, safety in,
  xxiii–xxiv
science tools, 25–31

to explore, 26–27
to measure, 27, 28–30
scientific inquiry, 13–19.
  See also Inquiry Skills
  classify and
    communicate, 16
  draw conclusions, 18,
    39
  hypothesize and plan,
    17, 37
  infer, 18
  make a model and
    sequence, 19
  observe and compare,
    14, 36, 40
  predict and measure,
    15
  test, 38
scientists
  how they work, 35–41
  think like a scientist,
    36–41
seasons, 253–261
  fall, 258–259
  spring, 254–255
  summer, 256–257
  winter, 260–261
seeds, 383, 397
seeing (sight), 7
senses, 3–7
  body parts, 4–5
  learning with, 6–7
sequence, 19, 74, 94,
  367

Set a Purpose, 11, 23,
  65, 79, 103, 155, 199,
  201, 247, 295, 331,
  353, 401
shadows, 286–287
shape
  for hiding
    (camouflage),
    348–349
  of leaves, 382
  as property of matter,
    92
shelter, 316
shrubs, 395
sight, 7
silt, 193
sink, objects that,
  96–97
size
  of leaves, 382
  as property of matter,
    92
sky. See also weather
  changes in, 285–291
  cloudy day, 290–291
  daytime, 274–275
  morning, noon,
    afternoon, 286–287
  nighttime, 276–278
  objects in, 271–279
  phases of the moon,
    288–289
  shadows, 286–287
  starry night, 290–291
  telescopes, 278–279
smell, 7
soil, 183, 190

© Houghton Mifflin Harcourt Publishing Company

Index

composition of, 190–195

formation of, 191

as natural resource, 183

properties of, 194–195

solar energy, 131

solids

    freezing, 106–107, 233–234

    melting, 108–109

sound, 125, 126–127

space. *See* Earth;
    moon (of Earth);
    star; sun

speed, 146

    changing, 146, 160–161

spring season, 254–255

star, 274

starry night, 290

stars, 277

STEM (Science, Technology, Engineering, and Mathematics)

    See the Light: Compare Flashlights, 297–298

    On the Farm: Farm System, 357–358

    Fly to the Sky: The First Flight, 169–170

    Kitchen Technology: Cooking Tools, 115–116

A Place for Animals: Keeping Animals Safe, 333–334

    Warm It Up: Compare Greenhouses, 403–404

    Weather Wisdom: Weather Tools, 265–266

stems, 381

straight line motion, 148

streams, 204

summer season, 256–257

sun, 274

    for energy production, 131

    morning, noon, afternoon, 287

    shadows, 286–287

    sunlight in food chain, 322

T

tadpole, 362–363

tape measure, 27

taste, 7

technology to predict the weather, 242–243

teeth, animal, 346

telescopes, 278–279

temperature, 95, 238

    freezing, 106–107, 233–234

hot or cold, 95

    measuring, 27, 103–104, 238

    melting, 108–109

testing

    in design process, 55, 60

    scientific inquiry, 38

texture, 92

    as property of matter, 92, 93

    of soil, 195

then, as clue word, 58

thermometer, 27, 238, 265

Think About the Procedure, 11, 23, 65, 79, 103, 155, 199, 201, 247, 295, 331, 353, 401

think like a scientist, 36–41

tools

    kitchen tools, 115–116

    science tools, 25–31

    telescopes, 278–279

    weather tools, 240–243, 265–266

touch, 6

trees

    described, 394

    fall season, 258–259

    oak, 394

    pine tree, 397

    seasonal changes, 255–261

© Houghton Mifflin Harcourt Publishing Company

spring season, 254–255

summer season, 256–257

winter season, 260–261

Tsui, Eugene, 81–82

tundra, 320

water, 203–211

condensation, 111

dams, for energy production, 130

for drinking, 208

for energy, 209

evaporation, 110

freezing, 106–107, 233–234

fresh, 204–205

keeping it clean, 209

melting, 108–109

as natural resource, 179

for plants, 209

pollution in, 218–219

as rain, snow, sleet, and hail (precipitation), 239

safety, 210–211

salt water, 206–207, 317

uses of, 208–209

water vapor, 110–111

weather, 233–245.

See also **seasons**

measuring and recording, 238–239

predict, 242–243

rain, snow, sleet, and hail, 239

rain gauge, 239

temperature, 238

watching, 236–237

wind, 240–241

weather balloon, 243

weather pattern, 254

weather plane, 265

weather satellite, 242, 265

weather station, 243

weather vane, 265

weight, 94

Why It Matters, 30–31, 74–75, 96–97, 164–165, 210–211, 224–225, 242–243, 278–279, 324–325, 384–385

wind, 236

for energy production, 131

observing and measuring, 240–241

wind farms, 178

windshield wipers, 45–46

windsock, 240

wind vane, 241

wings, 345

winter season, 260–261

Wright, Wilbur and Orville, 169

zigzag motion, 148

zoo keeper, 371–372

© Houghton Mifflin Harcourt Publishing Company